Endorsements

What started as a quick meeting with Joanne turned into a deep friendship with my family. Joanne and her husband are not ministry connections; they are friends. Anyone can sit behind a desk, write, and theorize about God's call and transformational process. Joanne's message is honed from years of study, her daily walk, and powerful testimony of Jesus working in her own life. The testimonies I have heard and witnessed firsthand speak of Joanne's walk with Jesus that evokes holy jealousy in my own life. Stop licking your wounds, get this message in your heart, and let Jesus transform you. *Everyday Supernatural* is not just another Christian self-help book; it is a call to action championed by a warrior who is tried and true.

—**Will Hart**
CEO of IRIS GLOBAL

I have absolutely loved reading Joanne's continuing journey of life in the Spirit in this book, and so will you, as it is filled with amazing stories and foundational biblical truths. I think my favorite quote from chapter 4 sums up her journey, "*It was as if a veil had been removed from my eyes and opened to the reality of what true Christianity looks like: Ordinary people doing extraordinary supernatural things because of Jesus and the presence of the Holy Spirit.*" This book is an invitation for you jump in and join what God is doing. The testimonies in it are calling out for God to come do it again. Freely you have received, freely give! The genuine love of (and for) Jesus and authenticity of Joanne and the Agape Freedom Fighters are inspirational, as God is calling every saint to join this quest to expand God's Kingdom. What more can I say—it's a great read!

—**Dr. Rodney Hogue**
Rodney Hogue Ministries

If you have never had the privilege of meeting my friend Joanne Moody, there is no better introduction than *Everyday Supernatural*. Like its author, the book is wonderful, powerful, and anointed. Each chapter is riveting (the snorkeling adventure had me anxiously holding my breath), enlightening, and convicting. It reads like fresh water in a dry and thirsty land. Like her first book, *Minute by Minute*, this is Jo's story and an invitation into our own miraculous, supernatural journey. Let this book, this word of the Lord, be written on your heart and emblazoned in your memory. The world is waiting for us all to grasp *Everyday Supernatural* ministry.

—**Dr. Kim Maas**
Founder/CEO Kim Maas Ministries
Author of *Prophetic Community: God's Call for All to Minister in His Gifts*, and *The Way of the Kingdom: Seizing the Times for a Great Move of God*

Joanne Moody is absolutely genuine. The encouragement she has brought to my wife and my life has been invaluable. I am so glad she has written this book, because this is a book born out of trial and genuine practice. We would not be where we are today without her voice in our lives. Her voice, now coming to you, is well worth buying and sharing. As every word has been paid for in practice and in Christ's presence. You will learn that Heaven, even in your trial, is a lot closer and more available than you think.

—**Parker Green**

"There's gotta be something more!" We've all wrestled with this tension as we have pondered the supernatural invitation given to us through the Holy Spirit. *Everyday Supernatural* by Jo Moody will ignite you with a fresh passion to risk, step out in faith, and live the wild life of miracles that is available to all who believe. What would be possible if every believer fully accessed all that God had for them? I believe that Jo Moody is the prophetic voice to our generation saying, "You can do it!" with boldness, humor, and raw transparency. I believe this book will not only encourage you but will catalyze you to move in the love and power of God in unprecedented ways!

—**Jessi Green**
Revivalist
Author of *Wildfires*
Director of Saturate Global

My life is separated into two parts—before and after I met Joanne Moody in April 2018, where Holy Spirit used her to radically heal a 20-year back injury, to speak into my true identity with deep inner healing, and to give me a prophetic promise that would come to fruition years later. There are thousands of stories similar to mine and the ones Joanne shares in this book—miracle moments all over the world where Jesus uses ordinary people to do extraordinary works, revealing that God is not looking for the perfect person; He is looking for the available one. Joanne's incredible sense of humor, strong biblical teaching, and never-changing focus on Jesus make this a book you simply cannot put down. I will be forever grateful for our friendship and the adventure we are on together to lift the Name of Jesus and speak life over His beautiful creation.

—**Kimberly Clarke**
Kingdom Ventures and Innovation

Jo Moody's book *Everyday Supernatural* is an inspirational read that will leave you hungering to see God radically move through your own life. With revelation, testimony, and humor Jo gives us an invitation to pursue the "more" that God has for each of us. One of the most beautiful things about this book, and Jo's life, is that it challenges the notion that God only wants to use a select few anointed people and instead exemplifies the opportunity for all of us to live a life of adventure with Holy Spirit. Whether Jo is preaching in a conference or at the gym, Jo authentically models a life of being "everyday supernatural" through the power of Holy Spirit. There are few I have met who live so intentionally to freely give what they have received as Jo does. I know that this book and her life will continue to ignite even more of us to live as yielded vessels for the love and power of Jesus to impact the world.

—Jessika Tate
Founder/President Yielded Ministries Global
Author of *Trials to Triumph*

Everyday Supernatural

Everyday Supernatural

EXPERIENCING GOD'S UNEXPECTED
MANIFESTATION IN
YOUR LIFE

JOANNE MOODY

DESTINY IMAGE® PUBLISHERS, INC.
P.O. Box 310, Shippensburg, PA 17257-0310
"Promoting Inspired Lives."

This book and all other Destiny Image and Destiny Image Fiction books are available at Christian bookstores and distributors worldwide.

For more information on foreign distributors, call 717-532-3040.

Reach us on the Internet: www.destinyimage.com.

ISBN 13 TP: 978-0-7684-6207-4

ISBN 13 eBook: 978-0-7684-6208-1

ISBN 13 HC: 978-0-7684-6210-4

ISBN 13 LP: 978-0-7684-6209-8

For Worldwide Distribution, Printed in the U.S.A.

1 2 3 4 5 6 7 8 / 26 25 24 23 22

*Be who God meant you to be
and you will set the world on fire.*

ST. CATHERINE OF SIENA

Dedication

For Parker, who is dearly loved,
and to your whole generation.

Acknowledgments

For all the things the Lord has done since my healing miracle in 2013, I am eternally grateful. To know our heavenly Father, to see Jesus face-to-face, and to walk with the Holy Spirit fills my heart to overflowing with thanksgiving. Without the Lord, this book would have no substance and no reason to exist.

Thank you, Mike Moody, my steadfast and adorable husband who married a force and instead of trying to tame her became the wind of love to propel her into her destiny.

To my beloved son, Kian, and my new daughter-to-be, Izzy— you inspire me to be a better mom and stir a hunger inside of me to bring Jesus to your generation in a tangible and irresistible way.

Huge thanks to my amazing administrator and dear friend, Kelsey King—with eyes like an eagle and the heart and wisdom of Solomon. What a gift from God you are.

To my dear friend Joanne Allyn for her ability to bring things to a point and hit the bull's-eye. Thank you.

To all of my friends and co-laborers for Jesus who took the time to review this manuscript and endorse it, my heart is grateful for each one of you.

To the family at Destiny Image and my friends Shaun Tabatt and Tina Pugh for their patience and for making this possible.

To Doreen and Scott Morehouse for your generosity to rest in your amazing desert home where this book began.

For Kimberly Clarke for filling my life with humor and making margin and rest possible for me.

Thank you to our Agape Freedom Fighters ministry and intercessory teams for being the hands and feet of Jesus all over the world. Your testimonies and your joy delight my heart, and my life overflows with love because of you.

For our AAETC (Agape Apostolic Equipping and Training Center) students around the globe: Many of you will write your own books and create a living account of the miracles of Jesus happening through ordinary people today. I cannot wait to read them.

To my spiritual daughters and sons, thank you for pressing into Jesus, risking it all with the Holy Spirit, running past me and doing more than I can even dream for you. You're all incredible.

To my PIA, Jessika Tate, it's roller derby time. Multigenerational revival!

Finally, for you, dear reader: Thank you for not only reading this book but for trusting that you are born for the "everyday supernatural" life in Jesus. Risk everything to love as He does and watch the Kingdom spread.

Contents

Foreword by Kathie Lee Gifford. 17

Foreword by Randy Clark 19

Preface. 23

1   Hidden Captivity 31

2   What Love Does. 43

3   Faith Like a Child. 65

4   The Power of Agreement 77

5   The Key of Forgiveness 91

6   Love as I Love You 105

7   The Truth about Trials. 115

8   Flying with Jesus 127

9   Horizontal People 141

10 A Word in Season. 157

11 The Unexpected 165

12 When Things Don't Make Sense 181

13 The Altruistic Life 191

14 God's Reflection 201

15 Overcoming.................................... 213

16 Obstacles Become Opportunity................... 229

17 Even Though You Are Tired and Weary............. 239

18 Opportunity Knocks............................ 253

19 Open My Eyes 271

    Afterword...................................... 281

    About Reverend Joanne Moody.................... 285

Foreword

In my lifetime I have met and observed and interviewed an untold myriad of extraordinary people from thousands of different walks of life. I hope along the way I've gained a little wisdom, too. I feel that I've grown to recognize the truth from the counterfeit, the real from the phony. People eventually reveal who and what they are. Now, it's certainly not my place to judge anyone—that responsibility belongs to God alone. But the Bible warns us all, *"Dear friends, do not believe every spirit, but test* [them]*"* (1 John 4:1 NIV).

It also says, *"Behold, I am sending you out as sheep in the midst of wolves; so be as wary as serpents, and as innocent as doves"* (Matt. 10:16 NASB).

So, when a friend told me an incredible story about a woman named Joanne Moody, I reacted the way I usually do. I was intrigued but skeptical. I've just seen too much that disappointed me over the years and been brokenhearted too many times by people who proclaimed to know and love God while the fruit of their private life told a very different story.

When I tell you that Joanne Moody is the real deal, I hope you believe me.

She is indeed a devout and devoted servant of the Living God. She does heal the sick. She does prophesy. She does command demons to flee and she has watched as the Holy Spirit has miraculously moved in countless lives, releasing them from a lifetime of brokenness. All because she prays. And because she has suffered so much for so long, Jo understands the pain of others in a way that very few of us could. And because she loved the One who redeemed her from her own indescribably agony—her Savior and the lover of her soul, Jesus—she has committed the rest of her life to working alongside Him to set others free. Free indeed!

Joanne is inexhaustible in her devotion and yet maintains a surprising "wicked" sense of humor. She delights in a God who loves laughter. And, yes, has been known to break into a Motown song with the voice of a soulful angel. With pretty impressive choreography!

I am honored to call her my beloved friend and sister in the Kingdom. And I'm thrilled that you are about to embark on an extraordinary journey into deeper truths that dwell in the spiritual realms. Take her hand. You can trust her. And just like Joanne, you too can experience *Everyday Supernatural.*

—Kathie Lee Gifford

Foreword

Joanne Moody's new book, *Everyday Supernatural: Experiencing God's Unexpected Manifestations in Your Life,* is filled with compelling accounts of the author's reliance on God and her supernatural encounters with Him after having battled through physical suffering for more than fourteen years. Including a near-death experience that clarifies the purpose of her long suffering, emphasizes the power of prayer, and encourages others never to give up hope. After having endured thirteen surgeries, Joanne is radically healed in an instant proving that God is a God of miracles and that His divine power accessed through faith can overcome all. *Everyday Supernatural* builds on her first book *Minute by Minute: A Story of Perseverance, Death, and the Miracles that Followed.* This sequel is one of the most fascinating books I have read and is full of stories of how to be led by God's Spirit, resulting in powerful healings and miracles. But it is not the story of Joanne Moody alone, it is more the story of the Agape Freedom Fighters. It is filled with the name of the teams of normal people that travel the world with Joanne in order to pray for people and equip people to be used by God to bring His love and compassion to them through His tangible miraculous power.

Everyday Supernatural is a joyous book. There is so much joy and delight, laughter and surprise that permeates the book as these normal, everyday laypeople discover the surprises of God through divine appointments, prophecies, and words of knowledge that reveal how

God is working with them to touch others. It is a book that brings hope and builds faith. I read most of the book in one sitting. It was hard to put it down.

Last week Joanne was one of the speakers with me at one of my conferences hosted by the largest traditional Baptist Church of 20,000 people in Brazil. Joanne is one of the most beloved prophetic persons who speaks into this strategic and significant church that is providing leadership to over 700 other churches.

Her story of how God anointed her in the prophetic and in words of knowledge was truly amazing. I have met few ministers who move in such prophetic revelation and who has such a passion for healing.

I have known Joanne ever since she was healed at our Voice of the Apostles conference in Orlando several years ago. I can vouch for her integrity. She is one of a select few who completed our *Christian Healing Certification Program* at the Master Equipper Level consisting of twelve eight-week master level courses equally divided into physical healing, inner healing, and deliverance. She took what she was learning and taught it in her 5,000-member mega church in California. At the time of her healing the church didn't believe in gifts of healing or in persons who had gifts of healing. She worked as an assistant to the lead teaching pastor. What a surprise to him when she returned no longer severely limited physically and in amazing health with her incurable condition healed. She raised up over 80 people in the local church who also began to see healing when they prayed. She is also ordained under the Apostolic Network of Global Awakening which I oversee. Her stories are not exaggerations. Joanne is the real deal. You can't take people with you and then exaggerate your stories for they were there to witness what happened.

If you want to have a quick, easy read that is extremely inspiring, and encouraging, you will enjoy *Everyday Supernatural.* If you would like to live a more abundant, victorious, supernatural life that brings joy, meaning, purpose, and humbling experiences of the presence of the Almighty God, *Everyday Supernatural* is for you. It will first, cause you to realize this kind of life is possible, second, it is available to followers of Jesus, third, you can actually learn how to cooperate with God by the stories that reveal how the team members discover what God is leading them to do not just in churches but in airports, grocery stores, and on the street. I consider Joanne an amazing spiritual daughter of whom I am well pleased. I hope she will follow up with another sequel to her amazing God-filled miraculous lifestyle.

—Dr. Randy Clark
D.D., D.Min., Th.D., M.Div., B.S. Religious Studies
Overseer of the Apostolic Network of Global Awakening
President of Global Awakening Theological Seminary

Preface

"NO EYE HAS SEEN, NO EAR HAS HEARD,
AND NO MIND HAS IMAGINED WHAT GOD HAS
PREPARED FOR THOSE WHO LOVE HIM."

1 CORINTHIANS 2:9

When I stop and think about what has happened since August 16, 2013, I am overwhelmed by the goodness and kindness of God. Never in a million years could I have dreamed of the plans God had for me. Prior to my miracle healing on that fateful day in August of 2013, I never pondered First Corinthians 2:9, perhaps because I could not envision it applying to me. Pain has a way of distorting truth. I had suffered in chronic pain with pudendal nerve entrapment for almost fifteen years. That, in addition to the complications resulting from thirteen surgeries, warped my perspective of God's greatness and His love for me. Despite what I read in the Bible each day, I had difficulty believing God loved me as I was. The more I tried to make sense of my suffering, the more I developed my own theology to support it—my suffering was a sort of penance to endure in order to purify myself from my worldly life before I met Jesus; and God was busy healing others more deserving than me. Even more insidious was the darker thought I kept buried deep inside—I somehow came to believe I suffered because I was not truly worthy of being healed. I was bound to these lies, which in turn kept me from having the faith to believe God had something great planned for my life beyond pain.

Today, I travel the world as an ordained minister of the Gospel of Jesus Christ with our Agape Freedom Fighters prayer team. I see these same lies embraced and believed by the Body of Christ everywhere I go, preventing the healing power of Jesus from bringing freedom from the bondage of affliction and oppression. The truth is, God knows our names. He knows our every thought. He created us and knit us together in our mothers' wombs. There is nothing hidden from Him. He took our frailties and diseases upon Himself so that we would be free. He paid the price for our salvation, sanctification, and restoration—body, mind, and soul. Sozo. His perfect love casts out fear and changes our perspective. When we know we are seen and loved by the Creator of the universe, who is perfect and unchanging, we can believe that He desires to heal us in our innermost parts (see 1 Pet. 2:24).

Recently, the Lord woke me up in the middle of the night, reminding me of the face of a young woman I had seen sitting in the second row of a conference we were doing in the United Kingdom. The Lord spoke to my heart, telling me her name was Rebecca. The magnitude of God's love for her seared an imprint into my mind and emotion. It overwhelmed me and remained when I began getting ready for day two of our conference. Because of the image and impression of God's love for this young woman, I called her up to the front of the gathering directly after worship on that second day. A look of shock moved across her face. She was sitting among a small group of young women who had been brought from a resident ministry house for those struggling with addiction and other life-controlling issues.

I said, "Is your name Rebecca?"

Wide eyes blinked back at me.

"Well, Rebecca, the Lord woke me up in the middle of the night with your face in front of me and told me how much He loves you."

She smiled, with a nervous glance at me, and shifted her weight from foot to foot. Her cheeks flushed crimson, and she lowered her head.

I squeezed her hand and asked everyone in the room to pray with me. As I spoke over her, the Holy Spirit gave me very specific words about her past, God's healing over every part of her life, and His promises of her future. I had never met this young woman before and could not have known any of these things prior to that moment but for the impressions of the Holy Spirit. With her permission, I led Rebecca through the prayers of forgiving the ones who had harmed her, as well as forgiving herself.

In the Name of Jesus, she verbally renounced the power of agreement with rejection, addiction, and unworthiness, as well as the belief that she was relegated to a life of failure and mistakes. The power of the Holy Spirit and the great love of God the Father fell heavily on Rebecca. She was moved to tears and began to shake under the power of the Holy Spirit while the entire conference prayed in unity with what the Lord was healing in her. Eventually, Rebecca fell down under the weight of God's glorious presence and, as she related later, had an amazing encounter with Jesus as she rested on the floor (see Acts 2:15; Ezek. 1:28). Her countenance was sheer joy when she was able to move back to her seat. For the rest of the day, she never stopped smiling and laughing. This is who she really is: a woman destined to bring encouragement and hope to others just by entering a room. Her smile lit up the room, and her laughter could be heard in the church lobby. What an incredible contrast to the bound, discouraged young woman I first witnessed! I could not contain my own overflowing gratitude to God for setting this young woman free.

The next day at the conference, one of the leaders of the ministry where Rebecca came from got up to share a testimony. She reported that the night before I called her up to the front at the conference, Rebecca had said to her, "I don't want to go back to the meeting. I don't even think any of this is real. Other people have things happen to them and they get called out, and I feel nothing. If God is real, He doesn't care about me. So, if He calls my name personally, then I will believe."

It was only hours after Rebecca's conversation with her house leader that the Lord woke me up. Putting her face before me, He prompted me to call her out first thing at the conference the next morning. This is how personal Jesus is. He hears every word and invites ordinary people like you and me to be the ones to release His healing love over those around us. What an extraordinary life we are called to live with Him.

Preface

Before returning to her seat. the ministry leader shared what happened to Rebecca after her encounter with the Lord that morning at the conference. Rebecca returned to her group home with all the others, where she prayed for and encouraged every young woman in the house. She stayed up late into the night worshiping and thanking God. She is a new person, with new thinking and new behavior. What a privilege to see a Holy Spirit makeover!

When we hear the Word of God, while encountering the Holy Spirit, it brings radical, personal transformation. Rebecca's past has not changed, but she reports that it no longer defines her. She now believes the person of truth, Jesus Christ, and what He says about her life. The Word of God says, *"You will know the truth, and the truth will set you free"* and whom the Son sets free is *"free indeed"* (John 8:32, 36 NIV). Jesus always preached the Word and prayed for those sick and spiritually oppressed. Throughout the Gospels, we read the accounts of each person who was brought to Him. One by one they were radically changed when they encountered the Messiah and believed (see Luke 4:23-24, 40; Matt. 15:30).

Like me, Rebecca received not only her emotional and spiritual freedom, but the divine revelation of the abundant life promised for us as believers in Christ through His Word and the presence Holy Spirit. Her spiritual eyes were opened because she felt seen and known by God through the words the Holy Spirit had given to me. These face-to-face encounters manifest all around the globe, as ordinary believers lay hold of the promises of God and bring the truth of the full Gospel of Jesus Christ to those suffering around us. This is what we are created for. This is the adventure we have been invited into—to help those afflicted and in need. John 14:12 says, *"I tell you the truth, anyone who believes in me will do the same works I have done, and even greater works, because I am going to be with the Father."*

Jesus tells us in John 10:10 (AMP) that *"the thief comes only in order to steal and kill and destroy"* but He came to bring *"life...in abundance."* Life in abundance refers not only to eternal life in Heaven, but also to our life here and now. Everywhere in the world where I have had the opportunity to travel, the deceiver is busy about his business of killing, stealing, and destroying. The distortion of the truth is the belief that it is God's will that we suffer. The belief that the promises of Jesus for our abundant life are only in our eternal heavenly state *steals* the destiny of our earthly lives and creates a powerless Gospel. Nothing kills hope more quickly than the assumption that we have no supernatural ability to create change here on earth and that we are simply biding our time waiting for Heaven.

The Word of God says that if we resist the enemy he will flee (see James 4:7). Some of us were never taught how to resist the enemy or to recognize the patterns of deception he uses against us. I know that was true for me. Maybe you are like I used to be before I was healed; not understanding what Jesus really paid for through His perfect sacrifice on the cross and His daily intercession for us. Perhaps you have never experienced our heavenly Father's love or the power of Jesus to heal through His marvelous Holy Spirit. Or, perhaps you have not seen into the depths of God's love for you.

Throughout the Gospels we read of Jesus bringing love where love had not yet arrived—to the prostitutes and outcasts. Jesus touched lepers, sat with sinners, and spoke their names in love. He invited them into a deep relationship with Him, as He continues to do for us. Theologian Beldon Lane, writes, "Divine love is incessantly restless until it turns all woundedness into health, all deformity into beauty and all embarrassment into laughter." We are far from perfect, but in John 8:12, Jesus said, *"I am the light of the world. If you follow me, you won't have to walk in darkness, because you will have the light that leads to life."* We don't have the light when we're perfect and get everything together. We have the light as soon as we say yes to Him.

Having said yes, we are now in the process of learning that His love is the answer to all that we need. The love of God is wide and high and long and deep (see Eph. 3:18). The more of His love we allow to heal us, the brighter our light shines because we no longer hide under a veil of unworthiness and insecurity. This is the life of a believer in Christ—to live in the majesty of the Almighty and believe that we are accepted just as we are.

I invite you now to join me on my journey over the past few years since my miracle healing. The Bible is alive and active, and the truth of Christ's authority and power is the same yesterday, today and forever. With the Bible as our guide, we will look at the transformational testimonies of those who have been set free by Christ's perfect love through the prayers of ordinary people like you and me.

I pray that as you read you will be inspired, filled with hope, and overwhelmed by God's healing love. I pray you will be willing to say yes to the life of freedom that He has planned for you, which is exceedingly and abundantly more than you could ever hope for or imagine (see Eph. 3:20). You were born for the supernatural life, and the Holy Spirit is here to bring Heaven to earth through you!

1

Hidden Captivity

YOU CAN NEVER DO KINDNESS TOO SOON,
FOR YOU NEVER KNOW HOW SOON
IT WILL BE TOO LATE.

RALPH WALDO EMERSON

Because of my father's military career, my family moved about every three or four years while I was growing up. My three siblings and I were about as fond of this upheaval as the fried liver my mom tried to make us eat most weeks. No matter what my mom told us we were having for dinner, we always knew when it was liver because while it cooked, noxious fumes overtook the house. We'd hold our noses and complain of the stench. There was no getting away from it. Moving was similar. Into the living room we would file, breaths held against the displeasing news as my father announced our next place of residence.

"This time, kids, we have a total of ten thousand pounds for household goods, so you know what that means."

The air escaping our lips sounded like tires had been slashed. Groans and high-pitched squeals echoed off the walls.

He continued, "Oh, come on. I know this is hard for everyone, but you are going to love it where we're going."

None of us believed him, but we soldiered on. At age seven when you are told you are allowed one hundred pounds for your personal items—you know which dolls, stuffed animals, and precious collectables stay behind. I realized much later that my parents were developing within their children an ability to make decisions and grasp that despite sentimental value or emotional attachment, sometimes we have to leave things behind.

Once settled in our new location—whether in Taipei, Taiwan, or Temple Hills, Maryland—my mom would begin the all-too-familiar management of her children. "Joanne, you and your brother go outside and don't come home until you've met a friend. Your sisters are already at the base pool meeting all kinds of people." She opened the screen door, and out we went.

My younger brother David and I looked at each other and sighed as she locked the door behind us. We sat on the curb just around the corner and out of the view of our new house, hoping some child would ride by on a bicycle so we could report we had met someone. It was awkward, and if you met my parents, you'd know—we had no choice but to persevere.

When you know there is no alternative but to move forward, you learn to move. We mastered resiliency and self-sufficiency, but even more valuable than that, we were shaped through being immersed in the wake of my mother.

My mom, despite the challenge of moving and managing four children, modeled the power of kindness and an ability to laugh easily to shift the atmosphere into joy. She was far from perfect and had a tendency toward bluntness and intolerance if we crossed the line, but she could not and would not hold a grudge or remain upset. Laughter was always her preference. Take care of business with loving confrontation and shift back into joy. She was splendid at it.

My father taught us that no matter a person's position, each one was valuable. From our parents, my siblings and I developed an ability to retain hope and embrace the new people we met. We worked on the shifting back to joy part, and sometimes we were even successful.

We moved from Taiwan to Montgomery, Alabama, in the mid-1960s when racial hatred and segregation under the Wallace administration was paramount. I was six years old. "Mom, why does that sign say, 'Whites Only?'" I asked her while we walked through downtown Montgomery.

"Honey, that should not be there, but some people believe we should separate people because of the color of our skin."

I was confused, having just moved from the orient where there were no such signs or rules.

Over the next several years I would hear of Dr. Martin Luther King and the march on Selma, Alabama, along with other monumental moments to overcome racial segregation instituted by the governor of Alabama. It was a brutal time.

First Corinthians 13:11 (AMP) says, "*When I was a child, I talked like a child, I thought like a child, I reasoned like a child; when I became a [wo]man, I did away with childish things.*"

By 1970, when I was nine years old, like all children, I observed a great many things around me but did not have the ability to interpret what I witnessed until I matured. I am forever marked by a journey with my mother and seven-year-old brother in that year.

We had been assigned to move again—this time from Maxwell Air Force Base and into a Montgomery, Alabama, suburb for the year of my father's service in the Vietnam War. Money was tight, and my mother decided to work for the United States Census to earn extra money. My sisters were doing after-school activities most days, so my brother and I would load into the back of the cobalt-blue wood-paneled station wagon and prepare for the long drive into the remote outskirts of Montgomery. Places we had never been before. David and I sat on opposite sides of the back seat, looking out the window as my mother drove off the main road onto a barely visible red dirt road with overgrown weeds. The car bumped along the pitted-out road, and David and I made noises to entertain ourselves.

"Uh-uh-uh-uh ar-ar-are weeeeee th-th-th-there yeeeeet, Mmmmmmmmmom?" David said as he burst out laughing when his question sounded like motorized hiccups.

Mom was concentrating and looking to her right, where she had a large map laid out on the passenger seat. "Maybe we're close. I think it's up ahead," she answered, braking the car.

"Do you know where you are, Mom?" I asked.

She rolled her window down and looked out. With her frosted hair, yellow sundress, and huge round sunglasses perched high on her nose, she reminded me of Jackie Kennedy. "Yes, we have to turn here."

The car tires groaned as she made a sharp left turn into what I could only observe was an enormous overgrown field with mile-high grasses and weeds shooting midway up the car doors.

Determined, my mother drove on until we came to a grove of trees with an ancient wooden shack—sagging like an old man's pair of pants. Even a belt would not have helped keep it upright. The front porch drooped so low in the center that it might have looked like a smile if not for the feeling of fear and sadness it had coming from it. It washed over me.

I stole another glance and viewed tattered rags hanging against the glass-less windows. There, an old woman sat in a dilapidated rocking chair.

My mom stopped the car a little way from the house, so she wouldn't have to walk through the highest weeds. "Joanne and David, you stay in the car. I have to do my job." Without turning around, she gathered a manila envelope and opened the car door.

David and I didn't respond, as mom had already jumped out.

"Yoo-hoo! Hello! US Census, ma'am!" Mom yelled as she waved and smiled.

The rocking woman did not respond. Instead, a middle-aged bare-foot man in stained overalls with one strap hanging down and a few days' growth on his face opened the rusty screen door and looked over at our car.

"US Census! I need to get a count from ya'll." Mom waved again.

The man moved toward the edge of the porch. "Yes, 'em, ma'am! Ya'll come on over, now." His voice was steeped in that Southern

Alabama drawl we had barely learned to decipher in the few years we'd been there.

"Thank you, sir. I won't take but a minute of your time," Mom answered as she walked toward the porch.

My brother and I had rolled our windows down completely, swatting flies and mosquitos as we peered out at our mother's kindness at work.

Despite the countenance of my mother, the old woman in the rocking chair never looked up. I couldn't tell how old she was.

"Think that lady is a hundred, Dave?" I asked my brother.

"I dunno. How long is this gonna take?" He twisted around in his seat.

"How would I know?" I looked back at the old lady.

Under her patches of barely there gray-white hair, her face looked like it had been weathered through a thousand storms. No one was home in her eyes. The man also averted my mother's glances at first. I had never seen folks like this. I felt sorrow to my bones because in my nine-year-old mind, I didn't realize I was witnessing the fruit of a life of oppression, inherited through generations of captivity.

We couldn't hear the whole conversation, but I saw the exchange. My mother's beautiful smile finally put the man at ease because I believe he must have sensed that she didn't judge them. In my observation of my mother, I don't believe she ever saw color—she saw valuable human life. The man went inside to get a book to show my mom, then continued talking with her for the next twenty minutes or so.

Mom reported to us once back in the car that these folks only had a record of the births and deaths of their family written in their Bibles, and that was what she was looking at. There were no hospital records or birth and death certificates. All life and death happened at home.

We didn't even own a Bible at that time because we were Catholic, so I was incredulous.

"What? Nobody has babies at a hospital, and what about when they die? Gosh, Mom. They look sad."

"It is the way it is, Joanne. We have to believe things will improve. We all just have to do what we can." That was my mom's practical nature. Not perfection but simply trying with all you've got. Especially, in the kindness and respect category.

Our US Census, recording the total number of people in rural Montgomery, would continue with my mother for the next several weeks, and David and I would witness the same types of engagements over and over. Sometimes there would be two to ten shacks together and more people to gather tallies from, but always, my mother greeted the households with graciousness, respect, honor, and dignity. Eventually, she was able to really engage openly and encourage them to share stories of their family. I wish I had been old enough to write them down.

Through the 1960s and even into the early 1970s, the remnant of slavery was still palpable. Even though I hardly understood segregation as a child, there was an atmosphere of hopelessness and defeat that would hang as thick as the breezeless Alabama summer. I could sure feel it. Today it has great significance for me.

As I reason like an adult over these memories, the overall feeling that remains with me today is that the people my mother met had been freed but remained in captivity because their experiences marked them, conditioning them to respond either in fear or through an emotional paralysis that rendered them mute. Their family history of persecution, violence, and pain wove through generation after generation. We are no different today.

Jesus said, *"If the Son sets you free, you will be free indeed"* (John 8:36 NIV). But when our past traumatic experiences, pain, or the wounds and history of our broken families have never been brought into the light of Jesus Christ, we will often be held captive by those events and history and remain unable to lay hold of the freedom Jesus paid for. I believe the Body of Christ has been given the charge to bring this freedom through the power and authority of Christ to people's lives. It is not to be left up to a single pastor or counselor to help those in bondage.

Isaiah 61:1 says, "*The Spirit of the Sovereign Lord is upon me, for the Lord has anointed me to bring good news to the poor. He has sent me to comfort the brokenhearted and to proclaim that captives will be released and prisoners will be freed.*"

When we help others stand in the light of Christ as powerful intercessors for their own families, we break the patterns of chaos, pain, and destruction that has held generations in bondage. With Jesus, past painful memories can be reinterpreted in His perfect love, rendering impotent the strongholds of those memories. Jesus commissioned all believers in Matthew 28:18-20 to go forth and do as He did, doing even greater things.

Don't let another day go by without inviting Jesus into every remnant of pain or hurt whether personal or something within your family line. As you pray, may you know *"the hope to which he has called you, the riches of his glorious inheritance...and his incomparably great power for us who believe"* (Ephesians 1:18-19 NIV).

What's Next Activation

Prayer for the Breaking of Generational Strongholds

Holy Spirit, I invite You to show me the places in my family line where the enemy has created a stronghold.

Help me, Lord, to repent of these things on behalf of my family now.

Take a few deep breaths here and wait for the Lord to bring anything up and pray the following prayer.

Father, I place the blood of Jesus as a wall of separation between my mother and father, grandparents, and great-grandparents, and me. I repent for the sins of the previous generations and break the power of the agreements of bondage and captivity that have come through the assignments of the enemy against us. I sever any curses spoken over my family or by my family by the blood of Jesus. I render the weapons of warfare powerless against us, and I command any and all spirits of darkness to leave now in the Name of Jesus Christ. I receive every blessing You have on my family line, and I thank You, Lord that I am free.

Lord, I place the blood of Jesus between me and my own children, grandchildren, and any future generations as a wall of separation shielding future generations from living under any ungodly covenants made through my own sin. I release every blessing that You have given me to give to them in the mighty Name of Jesus. Thank You, Holy Spirit for filling me and blessing my entire family line.

For Personal Breakthrough from Captive Thoughts

Holy Spirit, I invite You to show me any memories that have become fortresses for the enemy to bring me harm.

Show me where there is any crack in my armor, Lord.
I will surrender all of this to You and believe that You
began a good work in me and You will see me through
to completion.

As the Holy Spirit reminds you of any memory, you do not have to relive it. Acknowledge that everything comes under the power and authority of Jesus.

Holy Spirit, thank You for bringing this to my mind. I
submit this memory under the covering of Jesus Christ
and I ask that You show me where You were in this
memory, Jesus.

Now wait again and look around in the memory to see if you can see where Jesus is. If He is not near to you in the memory as you watch, and you are comfortable asking Jesus to come closer, pray this:

Jesus, would you come closer? Jesus, what is the lie I
believe about this situation?

If forgiveness for someone or yourself, is needed, do that. If you need to break an agreement with a lie that you believed, say this:

I break agreement with...

If you were told your voice didn't matter, or you were worthless, pray:

> *Jesus, I forgive _____. My voice matters, and I am important. I will no longer remain silent and live in fear of man.*

Now ask:

> *Lord Jesus, what is the truth about me?*

Listen and watch.

> *Jesus, I receive Your truth. This is who I am and how I will walk forward. I am free now to leave this memory, this pain in my past. Would You take me to a new place with You?*

Watch and listen as you go with Jesus to a new place. This new place with Jesus becomes the memory to replace the pain—*"beauty instead ashes...joy instead of mourning"* (Isaiah 61:3 NIV). Meditate on the goodness of God and how loved you are in this moment and allow this to become your focus each day. As you have experienced freedom, giving it away to someone else spreads the Kingdom of Heaven.

Give It Away

When you think about what you've learned and experienced in this encounter here, ask the Holy Spirit to bring someone to mind who is held captive by their thoughts or family background. Now ask Holy Spirit how you can partner with Him to bring them into freedom and healing. Journal what you think, hear, have impressions of, or feel. Now, what will you do in response?

2

What Love Does

GOD GRANT ME THE SERENITY TO ACCEPT
THE PEOPLE I CANNOT CHANGE, THE COURAGE
TO CHANGE THE ONE I CAN, AND THE
WISDOM TO KNOW IT'S ME.

ANONYMOUS

Love changed the world and the history of the human race through Jesus Christ. Perhaps you already believe that because Jesus Christ is your Lord and Savior, or perhaps you have yet to trust that Jesus is who the Bible says He is: the only way to God. No matter where you find yourself at this moment, as you read on, I pray your heart will be moved and experience either knowing Jesus for the first time or discovering a relationship with Him in a deeper and more intimate way. John 3:16 (NKJV) says, "*God so loved the world that He sent His only begotten Son, that whosoever believes in Him should not perish, but have everlasting life.*"

For the first 18 years of my Christian walk, I heard most people focus on the eternal life in Heaven with God and rarely heard anyone make any reference to the supernatural power and authority we have all been given through our simple faith in Jesus. Much later in my Christian life, I began to comprehend what it means to live in a supernatural reality.

Praying to the Father on our behalf, Jesus said this in John 17:21: "*I pray that they will all be one, just as you and I are one—as you are in me, Father, and I am in you. And may they be in us so that the world will believe you sent me.*" I could go into an entire book about what Jesus meant in this entire section of John chapter 17, but I'd like to bring one point to light. We cannot be separated from God. We have been made one with Him in the unity of the Holy Spirit through the perfect sacrifice and position of King Jesus.

There is a great Hebrew word used in Genesis 1:26 (NASB) that I hope will help articulate what Jesus is praying in John 17: "*Then God said, 'Let Us make mankind in Our image, according to Our likeness.*'" The Hebrew word for image is *tselem*. The Hebrew word *tsel* comes from *tselem*, and it means "shadow." Our shadows mimic everything we do. They are visible when the sun is bright, and we stand in a specific direction of the light. The Hebrew word *tselem* (image) is meant to encapsulate the reflection of the whole human soul. This word includes all of what we hold within our heart and what we think about.

Through Jesus Christ we have this incredible inheritance, a priceless gift to be image-bearers of God, able to overcome the world and live and behave like God intended us to—to mirror what God is doing, just as our shadow mirrors our own movements in the light. You cannot separate a shadow from a person except to intercept the light that causes the shadow to be visible. Jesus said we are one with Him; we are His image, His shadow, and we cannot be separated.

There is no limit to the depth of the love and encounter we are invited to have with God throughout our earthly lives. Unless we create it, there is never a cap or ceiling to the fullness of the presence and power of the Holy Spirit available to us through Jesus Christ.

The barrier to experiencing more of His love and moving in the supernatural gifts of the Holy Spirit is usually fear. No matter where I travel in the world today, human beings have a standard of framing our personal values based on what we have accomplished, our social status or lack thereof, the amount of money we obtain or never obtain, our political positions, or even the position we have in our families. The list is endless. We categorize and reposition ourselves throughout our lives to advance according to the world and its systems. Without a supernatural perspective, we are destined to spend the majority of our time, energy, and resources on worldly endeavors while remaining apathetic, unchanged, and stagnant in our Christian lives and personal relationship with God.

To begin to understand living with a supernatural perspective we must face a reality. Earth is not our home. We are here for a very specific purpose. As I mentioned earlier, we are made in God's image as written in Genesis 1:26. Read the rest of Genesis chapter 1. There you will see the creation of mankind for a specific purpose: to take dominion over the earth and to rule over the earth as a co-heir with God. We do that through the authority and power of Jesus Christ.

I understand if you didn't grow up in this teaching, it can be a lot to comprehend. After all, you know yourself pretty well, right? I do too. We are just people. But, the Word of God says we are born again from above with a new nature. The new nature is the supernatural nature of Jesus who was fully God and fully man. We are the image-bearers of God, and therefore through Christ we have a supernatural inheritance in Him. We are here on earth as God's children to release the Kingdom of Heaven everywhere we go. We are not living here simply waiting to board the flight to Heaven. If you and I adopt a Christianity that subscribes to waiting to go to Heaven as the totality of what Jesus has done for us, we have missed the assignment and, I might add, the adventure. You were born to do greater things than even Jesus did, and if that were not true, He would not have said it.

Before I understood my own value in Christ, I sought the very things everyone else does. Striving was a way of life. I was so performance and success driven that I held three careers at one time through my twenties. I was a workaholic, driven to succeed at all costs because failure was not an option. I had no idea of the value of human life and certainly not my own. I began searching for God earnestly in my late twenties, and at the age of thirty-one I encountered God in the ocean off Oahu, Hawaii. This experience gave me a whole new perspective on the magnitude of God.

I'd lived in Hawaii for fifteen years, most of which was spent working. My friend and fellow musician Rory called me one afternoon in between jobs.

"Hey, Jo! Chris and I are going free diving on Wednesday. Isn't that the day you only work at the radio station? We aren't gigging that night."

"Um, yeah, Ror. I am off in the daytime, but I have songs to write and stuff to prep for my clients at the gym. So, I'll pass."

"You know what? You never come anywhere with us unless it's work. Have you ever even been free diving?"

"Nope. I have never been free diving, and if it involves killing things, then I'm seriously not going."

Rory laughed. "Come on, Jo. You don't have to spear anything. Just come with us. We want to hang out with you, and it'll be good exercise. That's a motivator huh?" My friend Rory was a salesman. He was also my Sunday morning triathlon training buddy. If I could get a rigorous workout, then he knew I'd consider it.

"All right, Ror. But I have to be back by five p.m. to be at the radio station."

"Great. Meet us out there at nine a.m. It won't be crowded. Everyone is working." He laughed and hung up.

I was sorry I said yes.

Wednesday came and I drove out to the Southeastern point of Oahu, winding through a neighborhood I knew but where I had never accessed the beach. When I parked my car and walked down a narrow path to the ocean, the view was breathtaking. There was no beach here, but jagged brown cliffs jutted out over the fiercely churning royal-blue sea below. The booming noise of the waves against the rugged bluffs coupled with the stark white foam created as the waves broke apart was enthralling.

"Hey! I can't believe you actually came." Rory smirked behind his sunglasses.

Chris nodded. "Good to see you, Jo."

"Good to see you too, Chris. No killing anything in front of me, okay? That's the deal."

Chris guffawed while he slapped Rory on the back. A man of few words, Chris went to the cliff edge and slipped on his dive fins.

"Let's go, Jo." Rory handed me a springsuit—a half-length wet suit—to slip on.

The rocks were hot, but I knew when the water got deep, it would be cold. We sat down, dangling our feet over the cliff face, and slipped on our three-foot-long dive fins. The fins made it much easier to get over the reef and out to the channel edge where Rory and Chris wanted to dive.

We stood up and jumped off into the churning water below. I was actually having fun. Chris had a little orange dinghy he was pulling behind him. It contained their fishing spears, bottles of water and bait. The plan was to spear octopus on the reef edge and barbeque it on the cliffs. I assured them I would be doing my own thing elsewhere since the only thing I ever wanted to kill was the cockroaches that seemed to be taking over the islands—they were as big as hamsters. Not really, but close enough.

We swam out for a long time in the beautiful, warm water until we could see the color begin to change and the reef ending. The channel just off the reef goes from dark blue to blackest black as no sunlight reaches the depth of the ocean floor in that area. The temperature change is also evident the deeper you go. I know what large ocean creatures swim in the channels off the Hawaiian Islands, so I opted to stay on the reef watching black-white-and-yellow angelfish swim around my legs. They were mesmerizing. With my dive fins I could stand straight up, see through my mask, and keep my snorkel out of the water while gently moving my fins back and forth underneath me. It was awesome.

I had just begun to try and talk to God a few months before this outing, even though I didn't really know if it was working because I never seemed to receive a response from Him. I knew about God in my Catholic upbringing and I believed Jesus Christ was God's Son, but I never read a Bible and didn't have context for anything despite my religious upbringing. I was so moved by the scene below me that it prompted me to say, *Wow, God, this is amazing! These angelfish are gorgeous! Look at the colors. They sure don't look like this at the aquarium, they are so much bigger and vibrant. Thank You for this day. I'm loving every minute of it.*

My peaceful bliss ended with a violent tug on my leg. My heart began beating out of my chest as a surge of adrenaline coursed through my body. My legs had drifted over the reef into the fathomless channel. Seconds before, I had been safe on the reef, and now anything was possible! I grew up in the era of the *Jaws* movie phenomenon, and my mind conjured up a great gaping mouth with huge teeth trying to take my leg off. Fear, like a gasoline fire, raced up from my belly and gagged me. Every morbid vision of being eaten in half flashed across my mind.

Get ahold of yourself!

Wave after wave of panic rushed over me. I was afraid to look toward my leg, but the tugging was fiercer than ever. I finally looked down, petrified to open my eyes. I expected to see the worst. Caught up in the fear cycle clouded my reasoning. There I saw Rory.

Why is he pulling so hard on my right leg?

With both of his hands frantically pointing while simultaneously thrusting his arms forward, I looked in the direction of his obsession.

What is that?

I witnessed a massive moving grayish brown wall.

The noises coming from Rory jerked me back into focus. He pointed over and over with his eyes as wide as a deer on the tracks looking at an oncoming train. Then I saw it—a giant eyeball looking at me! My mind was racing.

Oh my gosh, this is a whale. It's a whale or a very large shark. What? We have to get out of here. This thing is huge!

Rory grabbed my hand and pulled me toward the giant gray-brown wall that was continuing to move slowly in front of us. *Massive* is an understatement. We could not see above or below it.

Like a slow-motion movie, the wall continued moving to the right.

I yanked my arm back and watched Rory stretch his hand out and flick barnacles off of the side of the most enormous creature God has ever created. That's the difference between Rory and me. He goes in for the full adventure while I hang back and observe before I move. My plan upon observing this creature was to flee and certainly not engage in barnacle picking.

What seemed like ten minutes was, in reality, probably less than five. We were incredulous, staring after the tail fin of the gigantic beast as it swished back and forth, causing a current that pushed us backward as it swam away from us.

Rory, Chris, and I rushed to the surface to talk.

Blowing the snorkel out of his mouth, Rory sputtered, "Can-can you believe that, Jo? What the heck! That was a humpback whale!" He was spitting water everywhere and bobbing up and down in excitement.

"That was the coolest thing ever. I'm following it." Chris swam away, dropping his dinghy anchor to the reef.

"I have no words, Ror. That was just nuts," I said. "I have never seen anything so big except the 777s that land on the reef runway at the Honolulu airport. How crazy is this?"

"Best day ever. I'm going after it too. You should come." Rory swam off next.

I just stayed put, marveling in what I experienced. I had lived in Hawaii almost sixteen years by this time, and I had never been in the water with something so huge. I had seen humpback whales breach off the south shore when I ran a wellness center on the coast, but they were pretty far out.

God, You have outdone Yourself today. That was incredible. Thank You for scaring me half to death and then making sure this was a day I won't ever forget. Wow. You sure are bigger than I know.

We'd been out in the ocean for many hours by this time, and I was getting fatigued. We were a considerable way offshore, and I decided to go in and rest. Rory and Chris never told me anything about the currents there, and within fifteen minutes of swimming, I realized I was still in exactly the same spot. I knew enough to swim across the current to prevent exhaustion, but this would take hours to swim close enough to the cliffs to try and figure out how to get out. My friends had also neglected to tell me how to exit, and it never occurred to me to ask since we just jumped off the cliff into the water to start. The muscles in my arms were maxed and cramping so much they were seizing into a bent position.

I kept trying to shake them out to move toward shore. I knew I was almost done with my strength. I had been a body builder for over ten years, and I knew my muscle fatigue levels well. Out of desperation, I decided to head for the cliffs nearest me. The waves were crashing over this spot with a ferocious consistency, but I knew waves came in sets, so I tried to swim in when there was a brief lull in the crashing. The current alone slammed me up against the rocks as jagged as glass. My wet suit slashed open across the shoulder and chest, my hands bled, and my heart raced.

The next set of huge waves came in, jerking me down into the surf and slamming me against the razor-edged rocks over and over again. I could not get my breath, and salt water filled my mouth—choking me. My mask and snorkel were jerked from my head in the aggression of surge. Because my wet suit ended at thigh level, my legs now bled from new cuts and abrasions.

Help me! I'm going to die here, God. I have no more strength. If You will just get me up on these rocks, I will serve You. I'll give You my life. Please, help me!

As soon as I said those words in my mind, a huge wave came and propelled me onto the top of the cliff face. I landed facedown, hacking and coughing, shaking from head to toe from complete exhaustion and overwrought by the fear that I almost lost my life. I burst into tears and lay facedown for a long time.

Thank You. Thank You. I know that was You. I would have drowned. I will do whatever You say. Thank You, God.

As the shaking lessened, I turned over and slowly sat up to face the water again. At that exact moment, a school of twenty to thirty black spinner dolphins popped up out of the water like contestants in a synchronized dance show. Just as they finished, the humpback whale breached out in the channel I had just come from. The sight was riveting.

God, this is a National Geographic special just for me, huh? I just can't believe it. You saved me and now You do this. Thank You doesn't even seem like enough. So just in case, I really, really am grateful to You.

A short time later, Rory and Chris came up on the same side of the cliff we had jumped in on.

"Hey, you guys, how'd you get out over there?" I asked.

"You just wait for a big set and when the largest wave peaks, you hoist yourself up," Rory said. "That's the only place you can get in from,

Jo. The rest will kill you. Surf's too strong, current rips all around here, and the rocks are too jagged."

"Yeah, I found that out."

"You okay?" Chris looked over my wetsuit and bloody legs and hands.

"Yep. I'll be fine." I explained to them about the dolphins and the breach of the humpback.

They told me all about the baby she was protecting on the other side and how she allowed them to swim around her without issue.

"Best day ever, huh, Jo?" Rory sat down on a towel, and the three of us stared into the sun and thought about all we encountered.

The book of Job has an amazing verse. I wouldn't find it until years later, but it brought me right back to that day with God and the humpback whale. *"But ask the animals, and they will teach you, of the birds in the sky, and they will tell you; or speak to the earth and it will teach you or let the fish in the sea inform you. Which of these does not know that the hand of the Lord has done this? In his hand is the life of every creature and the breath of all mankind"* (12:7-10 NIV).

For many of us, God's creativity and magnitude is first revealed in nature. I was never the same after my whale experience. I gave my life to Christ within that year and on the same day as Rory. Ironically, we were in two different places that day and both encountered the love of Jesus in such a confirming way, we could no longer delay in being His. We were made new creations in Christ. The Word promises that.

Sanctification is defined as "the process of being made holy through the merits and justification of Jesus Christ through the work of the Holy Spirit." I agree fully and believe we are made holy the moment we receive Jesus as our Lord, but we aren't yet aware of the fullness of what we have been given. The process of being made holy by the power of the Holy Spirit happens when we allow the transformation process to occur so that we are enlightened more and more of every gift, purpose, and identity given to us through our Savior Jesus Christ. Sanctification brings about new ways of thinking through the means of healing. Our understanding of holiness, therefore, comes by knowing and experiencing God with greater intimacy. That's the life hidden with Him (see Col. 3:3).

Even after my whale adventure and giving my life to Jesus, I still had the compulsion to drive myself to be the best in whatever I was doing. The process of being a new creation was underway, but I was far from being healed from performance orientation. The drive to succeed did not evaporate overnight. But because I had experienced God in a supernatural way, I could no longer deny He was active in my life. As I moved into the weeks and months after my whale encounter, I had a revelation. Instead of launching into my life with my usual ferocity, I began to pray and contemplate what drove me. I wasn't in competition with others; I never liked team sports. I realized my competition was me. The internal force that compelled me to do more came from a place that had been there for as long as I could remember. I just didn't know that internal force was born of fear. Fear of being rejected by my father or mother for failing. For most of my life, I'd lived with a belief that I was a disappointment to my father. So, I learned to navigate the rejection issues by continuing to excel. As a method of survival, I shoved all manifestation of fear to the bottom of my being.

As I continued to grow in my relationship with the Lord, He began to teach me who I was in Him, but then everything shifted on August 16, 2013. I went from being a person who believed fully in Jesus Christ to a child of God transformed by His supernatural power and authority. I met God in a way I had never experienced. I often think of that moment when Heaven touched down on me, and I am moved to tears every single time. The Holy Spirit crashed into my mind, body, and soul through the prayers of a marvelous man named Richard Holcomb.

In less than fifteen minutes I was miraculously healed through Richard's determined prayers and the power of the Lord Jesus Christ. I bid good riddance that night to chronic debilitating nerve pain and the effect of thirteen surgeries in fourteen and a half years. Because of the power and authority of Jesus Christ and the presence of the Holy Spirit, Richard led me through a healing prayer to audibly break the lies I believed about God and about myself. Any residual rejection from my father and my position of self-rejection were addressed through forgiveness and the breaking of my agreements. Through the presence of the Holy Spirit, my thoughts of being unworthy to be healed were annihilated.

As I prayed with Richard, the power of my free will brought about the fullness of what Jesus paid for with His life. The right of the demonic to bring affliction, trauma, and even premature death was removed and the unbearable pain that had plagued me for more than a decade disappeared. Even to type those words today—eight years later—I am in tears. How wonderful God is! He also delivered me of opiate and benzodiazepine dependency at the same moment of my healing, and I suffered no withdrawal symptoms. The power of Jesus Christ and the presence of the Holy Spirit overshadowed me with immensity, and I was healed—mind, body, and soul. I am an anomaly to my doctors and surgeons.

I tell them and anyone who will listen: The glory of God is a weighty force, and His love feels like something. The Hebrew word for *glory* is the word *kabod*, which means a heavy weight. That's exactly what God's presence is. There is power when the Holy Spirit comes. I was not only radically healed, but I instantly knew that I was loved. The wraparound presence of the Lord's love is unlike anything else. His love transforms everyone who will accept it. We are unconditionally approved of, and there is nothing we can do to earn an increase. This adoption, the fullness of the Lord's embrace, is given to us freely. Jesus made it possible.

After my life-altering encounter of healing, I began to wonder how was it I had lived 18 years as a born-again Christian, even growing up going to church, and I never knew I could have access to the Lord like this before? I know now that I was never taught about intimacy with Christ but rather duty through religious practices. Because of this, I applied my performance-based value system to my Christian walk and missed God's grace entirely. If I was supposed to read three chapters of Scripture for my daily reading, I would read double that. I did countless Bible studies and learned all that I could. I memorized tons of Scripture and became a worship leader. I wrote songs about the greatness of God and loved God with all of me. But I couldn't receive the fullness of His love because I didn't think or feel any more valuable despite what I read and sang.

After my miracle healing, I realized that despite Richard being a successful businessman from Texas, he was an ordinary man. But God moved powerfully through him. Richard carried and released the extraordinary love of Jesus through the powerful demonstration of the supernatural presence of the Holy Spirit. Richard walked in miracles and wonders as a signpost of who Jesus really is. It was as if a veil had been removed from my eyes and opened me to the reality of what true Christianity looks like: Ordinary people doing extraordinary supernatural things because of Jesus and the presence of the Holy Spirit.

I decided to learn to do what Richard did and what Jesus said I would do. I enrolled in the Global Supernatural School of Ministry's Christian Healing Certification Program. There I discovered the sanctification process of becoming all that Jesus said we are is ongoing. That may not be news to you, but for someone who was performance driven and goal oriented most of my life, I had to learn to embrace the *journey* of sanctification rather than the *goal* of arriving. Not an easy thing for me.

I desired to do everything for the Lord, in the Lord, and focused on the Lord all day, every day. I was wearing myself out with work, ministry, and school, and I had a difficult time believing I had a right to rest. I had to actively contend against the familiar pattern trying to creep in and take over. Performance orientation was still there. But this time, I knew the Lord would help me get rid of it.

During that season, in a time of deep intimacy with the Holy Spirit, I closed my eyes and asked, "Lord, show me when I first made a decision that I had to be perfect and excel in everything I start. You know I still get tripped up into striving, and I want to know where that started."

I saw a vision almost immediately of me as a three-year-old and my father yelling for me to come over to him. I was dressed in a white flowered dress with white shiny leather Mary Jane shoes and white tights. It looked like something my mother would dress me in for church. My eyes were wide, and I was up against a wall—frozen. I didn't come when my father yelled because I was afraid.

He was yelling about getting into the car. When I didn't come to him, he came and picked me up, turned me over his knee, and spanked me hard. "Get in the car!" he yelled a final time when he was finished spanking me.

Seeing my little tear-streaked face, I felt a huge lump in my throat and a knot in my stomach.

In the vision I heard myself say to myself, "He doesn't love me. I will have to be better so Daddy isn't mad anymore." I asked the Holy Spirit to show me where Jesus was in the room when my father was spanking me.

Jesus was right beside my father and slid His own hand between my father's hand and my backside to lessen the impact. Jesus had tears in His eyes too. I was overwhelmed with His love and protection for me.

> *Jesus, thank You for being there to protect me. Thank You, Holy Spirit, for showing me when I decided my father was not trustworthy to protect me. I am grateful I see now that I vowed I must do everything myself and I believed my father would never support me.*
>
> *I choose to forgive my father for losing his temper so often and making me feel unloved and unworthy. I release him from the debt he owes to me and I ask You to forgive me for judging him. I break every agreement with the lie that I am rejected, I must always be self-reliant, and I will never be protected by the men that are in authority around me. I break the judgment against my father and all men in authority and I command the spirit of rejection, the spirit of performance, and the spirit of perfectionism to leave me now in the Name of Jesus Christ.*
>
> *Thank You, Lord, for freedom from striving. When You set us free, we are free for all eternity. Holy Spirit, please come and fill every place within me that once held onto lies and darkness. Thank You, Lord.*

While that was the last time I remember ever being spanked by my father, his yelling was a way of life. This reinforced my fear and eventually bitter root judgments that I could never make him happy or trust him to support me.

When a root judgment exists, it *"grows up to...defile many"* (Hebrews 12:15 NIV). Born of fear and reinforced by decisions and circumstances, these judgments become fortresses of belief systems deep within us. When not healed by the power and love of Jesus, these judgments and fears continue to shape us and rule us no matter how old we are. Even when our parents pass away, or people are no longer in our lives who reinforced these warped belief systems, we can still be driven by the fears because this way of life has become a stronghold of thinking. A stronghold is a fortress created for safety. Yet without Jesus being invited to heal us, the stronghold becomes a prison. Many times, bitter root judgments open a door for demonic oppression. The demonic oppression attached to a spirit of rejection simply reinforces the stronghold.

To tear down strongholds, we must have truth. Truth lies in understanding and embracing our value in Jesus Christ.

The discovery of our value will never come through head knowledge alone. There must be an encounter with the person of love who freed humanity. There must be relationship and transformation through the Holy Spirit of God (see 1 Cor. 2:6-16). We can make up our minds to believe in Jesus but to trust Jesus requires our hearts to be involved.

Jesus said to His disciples before His death, *"Nevertheless, I tell you the truth: it is to your advantage that I go away, for if I do not go away, the Helper will not come to you. But if I go, I will send him to you"* (John 16:7). Other versions speak of the Holy Spirit as Counselor, Comforter, or divine helpmate. He is all of those things and more.

Only through a deep and abiding relationship with Jesus through the Holy Spirit can we understand our true value. It starts here.

John 3:16 (TPT) says, *"For here is the way God loved the world—he gave his only, unique Son as a gift. So now everyone who believes in him will never perish but experience everlasting life."* We begin to understand the standard by which God the Father measures our value only in connection with His perfect love. Through the immeasurable love of the Father—who made a way for us from the wages of sin to the restoration of our birthright through the perfect sacrifice of Christ—we are no longer slaves but fully restored through faith in Jesus to our rightful place as children of God. As children of God, we are given full access to the relationship with the Holy Spirit. *"But those who embraced him, and took hold of his name were given the authority to become **who they really are**—the sons of God!"* (John 1:12).[1] To become our true selves. Fully restored to the Father through Christ.

Again, I bring to you Jesus' words in John 17: *"That they may all be one; just as You, Father, are in Me and I am in You, that they also may be in Us, so that the world may believe that You sent Me. The glory which You have given Me I also have given them, so that they may be one, just as We are one; I in them and You in Me, that they may be perfected in unity, so that the world may know that You sent Me, and You loved them, just as You loved Me"* (verses 21-23 NASB).

His love saves, heals, delivers, and frees every part of us. We are one with Jesus, God the Father, and the Holy Spirit. Therefore, our value is not ever determined by what we do. Our priceless value is determined by Christ's perfect, flawless identity that is in us. Together we are one Spirit with access to our full inheritance of His authority and power. We belong to the essential nature and constitution of God. God is Spirit and He is sovereign. He has absolute authority over all the universe and everything in it. He is not constrained by time or by space. He is immutable—the same yesterday, today, and for all time. He is the essence of love. He is limitless. You are His beloved offspring. With these realities in mind, it is time to invite the Holy Spirit to reveal any areas of doubt, disbelief, or other issues that prevent us from believing we are the perfect, beloved children of God, inheritors of the fullness of His power and authority. Ready?

— *Prayer* —

Holy Spirit, I want to know You better. I long for intimacy with You, Jesus. I desire a rich and abiding relationship with You, heavenly Father. Holy Spirit, show me what is hindering me from believing I am who You say I am.

What's Next Activation

When the Holy Spirit reveals something to you, act. Forgive where needed, including yourself. Repent, break agreements or unholy vows all in the Name of Jesus. If any oppressive spirit is revealed, make it leave in the Name of Jesus. Ask the Holy Spirit to come and fill you up with perfect shalom peace and for the joy of the Lord to be your strength. The Bible says where two or more believers are gathered, the Lord is in our midst. If you need help with prayer, please ask the Lord for a safe person in your life to invite into praying with you.

Staying Free

The practice of staying free requires discipline. Renew your mind as part of your daily focus. *"Finally, brothers, whatever is true, whatever is honorable, whatever is just, whatever is pure, whatever is lovely, whatever is commendable, if there is any excellence, if there is anything worthy of praise, think about these things"* (Philippians 4:8). With this Scripture in mind, actively replace the thoughts and words of judgment, fear, criticism, and rejection with words of truth, purity, and loveliness. I always tell myself and others, "If it is not a pure, noble, right, admirable or lovely thing why are we talking about it?" I know, it is easier said than done but in time the process of what your mind gravitates to will change from fear to victory. New patterns are built up by the power of the Spirit through spiritual discipline. This includes tearing down every lofty opinion raised against the knowledge of Christ.

Second Corinthians 10:3-5 in *The Passion Translation* says,

For although we live in the natural realm, we don't wage a military campaign employing human weapons, using manipulation to achieve our aims. Instead, our spiritual weapons are energized with divine power to effectively dismantle the defenses behind which people hide. We can demolish every deceptive fantasy that opposes God and break through every arrogant attitude that is raised up in defiance of the true knowledge of God. We capture, like prisoners of war, every thought and insist that it bow in obedience to the Anointed One.

Doesn't that hit home? We capture our rogue thoughts like prisoners of war! We take captive those thoughts that diminish the power of God to move on our behalf! I pray you realize as I have—when we war from this powerful place of truth, we are warring in alignment with the Spirit. When the enemy seeks to devour the children of God, it is first through doubt, confusion, and fear. When you feel powerless to change the way you think, just begin praising God. Sing or read Psalms aloud about the glory of God. Make that your response to anything uncomfortable and soon you will find greater hope that leads to faith in action. Be persistent. Be consistent. You are a powerful, supernatural change agent. Put on your spiritual armor and stand firm. When you have done all you can, remain standing. Resist the enemy and he will flee. The enemy will grow weary of harassing one who will not eat his fear bait and move onto another more easily led astray.

Give It Away

What did the Holy Spirit teach you this week? Who will you share it with? How will this impact you being willing to pray for them?

NOTE

1. Brian Simmons, *The Story of Jesus and His Love for You* (Racine, WI: BroadStreet: 2015).

3

Faith Like a Child

ANYTHING IS POSSIBLE,
ANYTHING CAN BE.

SHEL SILVERSTEIN

In the winter of 2015, I found myself in the middle of thousands of people trying to cram into a small church in a little country town in the south of Brazil. It was my second mission trip to Brazil with Global Awakening, and it felt like being with family. I was healed at the Voice of the Apostles conference in Orlando, Florida, through the ministry of Global Awakening, in August 2013. I took my first international trip with Global Awakening in December 2014. I found ministering in Brazil to be a dream come true. On that first trip, I witnessed God heal hundreds of people, including several cases of stage-four cancer. My faith on this second trip was high.

That day, we had ridden a bus for four hours to conduct a healing meeting outside of Londrina, Brazil. The air was thick with humidity, the heat was oppressive, and sweat ran down my face. I looked around and saw the crowds pressing into the church like a surging sea. More people standing outside were crushing through the doors to try to find a way in. Children, elderly, the wheelchair bound, teenagers walking with crutches, and several people with wild-looking eyes bent over muttering to themselves, were pressed into every available space and against the walls. Friends and family carried sick babies and supported frail parents. The need for Jesus was overwhelming.

As worship began, the heart of passion for Jesus rose up from all of those gathered as a collective cloud of devotion. My friend and fellow pastor, Blaine Cook, spoke of the great call for all people to come into the Kingdom of God—not because we are qualified but because we are called.

"I tripped into the Kingdom. If I can get in, then anybody can get in! Do you know how loved and powerful you are? The Holy Spirit is here, and Jesus wants to heal you!" As the translator spoke his words in Portuguese, a roar went up from the crown.

"Hey, prayer team, you have to pray using two hands!" Blaine yelled from the platform over the crowd.

I was confused.

"Hey, JoJo, like this!" he yelled to me, with his two hands in the air, pantomiming laying one hand on one person while placing the other hand on the person next to them. He was asking us to minister two people at a time. The crowd was too large to attempt the laying on of hands any other way.

The palpable presence of the Holy Spirit was everywhere, and the awesome, weighty glory of God brought a measure of faith that swept the room. Still, to pray for two people at the same time seemed daunting to me. I was accustomed to speaking to the people I prayed for, looking directly into their eyes, feeling the love Jesus has for them while praying for their healing. I had never done what Blaine was asking us to do, and I wondered for a second if he ever had either.

Even if we lack understanding, there is so much that God can do if we just move forward. I know His ways are higher (see Isa. 55:8), but I still ask questions. *How is this possible, Lord? How can I pray for two people with different illnesses, at the same time, with only one interpreter, while moving through this crowd?*

Before I could listen for a response, two people wanting prayer appeared in front of me. With a throng of more than fifteen hundred pushing in, I would be crushed if I didn't get moving.

"What do you want Jesus to do for you?" I asked.

The interpreter spoke to them and reported both were suffering from migraine headaches and both had a headache at that moment. They wanted Jesus to heal them.

What a weird coincidence. "Do they know each other?" I asked the interpreter.

As she spoke to them in Portuguese, they shook their heads no at me.

At that moment, I was torn between the supernatural and the natural. My mind raced to find logic and connection in the natural to explain how two people with the same afflictions could approach me at the same time. Meanwhile, I found myself drawing on faith to believe Jesus would do the impossible.

There is always a choice. I chose to lay down my desire to figure out just what was happening here through logic and reason, and instead focused on Jesus' amazing love and desire to heal the ones in front of me despite my inability to comprehend how this was happening. I placed one of my hands on each of the women's heads and commanded the headache pain and cycles of migraine to go in the Name of Jesus Christ. Immediately, both women were healed of all pain. No one was more shocked than me. We all shouted thanks to Jesus before I moved on through the crowd with my interpreter. As I left, I asked them to pray for healing for the people around them.

These two women laid hands on those next to them and prayed as they had just been prayed for.

Faith in action.

The world over, I witness the extraordinary manifestations of healing in the Name of Jesus through childlike faith. I have observed that when a person is healed by God and, in turn, prays for another afflicted person, the rate of healing is extremely high. Jesus said, if we have faith as small as a mustard seed, we could tell a mountain to move (see Matt. 17:20). Those who have just been touched and healed radically by Jesus experience such extreme faith that mountains of sickness can move from the ones that they, in turn, pray for (see Matt. 21:21). I never tire of watching the look of surprise on the faces of those who have just been delivered from sickness and oppression as they pass on what they have just received from Jesus.

As I inched my way through the crowd, I simply trusted the Lord in the moment and prayed for the people He put before me. His humor at times like this never ceases to amaze me. The next nine sets of people I prayed for were just like the first set of people—none of them knew each other, and yet they all shared the same affliction as the one they were standing next to for prayer. My fear of being unable to pray for two people at once proved ridiculous. He is, after all, Jehovah Rophe, God our healer. With His limitless creativity, He heals in ways that break every previous paradigm.

I was laughing and dumbfounded as 90 percent of all the people I prayed for were healed simultaneously. I had never been part of anything like it. God was doing something new in that moment, and I nearly gave in to fear because of my lack of understanding, rather than to surrender to Him in childlike trust. I am so grateful to the Holy Spirit for His guidance despite my lack.

The crowd was beginning to thin, allowing us to catch our breath, when I saw an attractive dark-haired woman approaching me holding the hand of a very small thin girl with long brown hair. The girl, who appeared to be about six years old, wore a little black-and-pink skirt with a black sleeveless shirt. As the woman and child walked toward me, I had a sudden vision manifest in front of my eyes. Almost like a dream, I briefly saw the little girl doing cartwheels all around the church in front of me. The vision quickly disappeared. I tucked it away as a possible key to something God was doing, as He was surely doing new things tonight.

The woman introduced herself to the interpreter. "I'm Claudia, and this is my daughter Pedrina. I would like for the lady [me] to pray for Pedrina's arm." Slowly Claudia rotated Pedrina so her left side was facing me. There I saw a malformed, completely limp arm without muscle, ligaments, or shape. It appeared that the arm was nothing but bone and skin. Her mother continued, "She was born this way, and her arm has no movement or feeling, but we believe Jesus will heal her tonight."

"I believe that, too." I smiled. After the last ninety minutes of praying for people and watching the power of God heal and set people free, I had faith on fire.

Before I launched into prayer, I heard the voice of the Holy Spirit, almost like an impression. Through intimacy with God and fasting, I have learned this is His voice and the most common way He speaks to me. He directed me to pray four times with short, very specific prayers. The Lord stirred in my heart that this was to be a creative miracle—the creation of a part of the body that was missing. I had never prayed for a creative miracle by myself, and I was so excited to see Jesus do the impossible because He does the impossible so well.

I began, "In the Name of Jesus, I command the re-creation of normal nerve conductivity in the brain, new neurons, and new receptors inside the arm, brand-new nerves created, and normal circulation in this arm. As it is in Heaven, let it be here now in Jesus' Name." I realized I was holding my breath and tried to relax.

The Holy Spirit continued to guide me, leading me to ask Pedrina to check her arm after each short prayer I prayed.

"Pedrina, can you move your arm?" I asked through the interpreter.

Pedrina said she could feel something hot inside her arm, and we could see twitching as her arm moved slightly back and forth.

"What? Come on! Okay, Jesus. Thank You, Lord!"

Pedrina's eyes grew wide. The interpreter moved closer into our circle. Claudia put her hand over her mouth.

I held my breath again, then I prayed what I was impressed by the Lord to speak. "In the mighty Name of Jesus and by His blood, I command every muscle, ligament, and tendon and all missing support pieces for normal movement of this arm to be created now."

Pedrina, Claudia, the interpreter, and I watched as her arm began to change shape.

I could not comprehend this with my mind. My voice was higher than normal. "Pedrina, can you try to move your arm again?"

The interpreter repeated the question in Portuguese.

We watched as Pedrina raised her arm to the side halfway up like the arm of a clock. Shock and amazement filled all three of us.

I prayed a third time for the neurological connections from her brain to her nervous system in activation of a normal functioning arm to be healed.

Pedrina raised her arm 75 percent of the way up. The arm looked more normal each time she lifted it.

The last directive I received from the Lord was to simply ask Pedrina to lift her arm straight over her head. "Sweetie," I said, "will you lift your arm straight up and give Jesus a shout of thanks?"

The interpreter asked the question, and we all witnessed the miracle of this little precious daughter's arm shoot straight up in the air as she screamed. Her mom, the interpreter, and I all screamed too. We were undone by the goodness of God, unable to process what we had just seen. Tears ran down our faces like rivers as we watched Pedrina leap into her mother's arms. Pedrina then threw her arms around her mother's neck, buried her face in her mother's neck, and sobbed. She had never before been able to hug her mom with both arms.

"Thank You, Father. Thank You, Jesus. Thank You, Holy Spirit." I could not stop thanking God and marveling at what I witnessed. He invited us into a front-row seat to marvel at the transformation of a beautiful little girl's life. God made this so simple for me, as He will for all who will partner with Him.

Claudia's tug on my arm brought me back into the moment. Through the interpreter she shared this: "Please, I must tell you why Pedrina asked me to bring her to this healing meeting tonight. She is the one who heard about it in our church last weekend when they said all of you were coming to pray for the sick. She told me she believed Jesus would heal her here because she wants to do gymnastics. Without the use of her left arm, that could never happen for her."

All I could do was smile, shed fresh tears, and nod as I was reminded of the vision of little Pedrina doing cartwheels as her mother brought her up to me for prayer.

How great and marvelous are the ways of God—they are beyond searching out (see Ps. 86:10; Rom. 11:33). I never grow tired of these surprise moments from the Creator of the universe—the great I Am who knows all things before we pray and loves with such extravagance. The way God personally loves and communicates is what our souls are built to experience. As believers in Jesus Christ, through the power of the Holy Spirit, we are invited into the story of God as His children, His co-heirs, His Beloved, Kingdom priests, and healing ministers of the Gospel of Jesus Christ.

Jesus clearly says that if we do not *"receive the kingdom of God like a little child,"* we will not enter it (Luke 18:17 NIV). The word for "little child" in the Greek, as it is used here in Luke 18:17, means "very young child," perhaps as young as a toddler. As I began an in-depth study on childlike faith upon my return from Brazil, I read the words in Luke 18:17 and responded, *Lord, that is ridiculous. Toddlers have no common sense, and they are out of control.* I could feel the humor of the Lord urging me deeper into my study.

In the days of Jesus, the disciples prohibited the children from coming to Him, believing children had no significance and were given to folly and forgetfulness. They were protecting Jesus' time and energy for men and women, their own idea of the ones who merited time and attention. Jesus is clear in correcting their thinking. It is not the child who needs to grow up to seek the presence of Jesus, but rather the man and woman who need to reduce themselves to a childlike state in order to truly find Him.

Children have faith, and the Bible tells us that it is impossible to please God without it (see Heb. 11:16). Young children possess humility, submissiveness, and a joy that is without limits. Small children are not weighed down by the world's concerns, or by what other's think of them. Toddlers are trusting and filled with exuberance for what is next. They love exploration and forgive without a second thought. Ugh. The words were like lightening to my forehead. The Lord was really getting mileage out of this study and driving home His point.

I recalled watching little ones play on the playground near my house. One moment a little boy with dirt-caked hands whacked a little girl in a pink sundress for taking his truck out of the sand. In the chaos that erupted, both burst into tears. Five minutes later, they were peacefully sharing cookies together. We can learn so much from them. Little children do not hold grudges or understand what it means to hold an offense. They love to express themselves with dance and song, art, and physical expression of every kind. They are affectionate and filled with wide-eyed wonder. I was beginning to understand the depth of Jesus' words that unless we come to Him as little children we cannot enter the Kingdom of Heaven.

As believers, the Kingdom is both within us and is also our eternal dwelling place (see Luke 17:21; Rev. 21:1-27). The Kingdom of God is righteousness, peace, and joy in the Holy Spirit (see Rom. 14:17). Matthew 18:3 tells us that we must become like little children to enter the Kingdom of Heaven and Jesus said the Kingdom had come upon those around Him. It's not the afterlife I am speaking of here but rather our lives in Him today. The key to entering into the supernatural Kingdom of Jesus—the righteousness, peace, and joy in the Holy Spirit—is embracing childlike faith. There is no greater expression of this truth than when toddlers play together. Peace and joy rule their hearts when they are in a safe environment. Even when conflict arises, upheaval is easily remedied with love and boundaries. I wish I had known this simple truth when I first became involved in ministry in my early thirties, where I watched those around me take offense, take sides, hold grudges, and divide churches. If only we had all been as little children.

The Kingdom of Heaven is God's eternal rule over everything, but it is also a spiritual rule over the hearts and lives of those who willingly submit to God's authority daily. With love and consistency, little children submit to authority fairly easily. This is something we all must learn to do. Jesus said His Kingdom is *"not of this world"* (John 18:36), and to be a part of that Kingdom repentance, as a lifestyle, is necessary (see Matt. 4:17). Toddlers very quickly turn away from things that are evil when they are protected by loving parents.

Coming to God with childlike faith requires practice and diligence. Seek Him in the quiet of the morning and in the still of the night. Be patient and know He is faithful to answer. Come to Him throughout the day with adoration, questions, thanksgiving, and worship. Learn to be a friend of God in every way by believing His word and His nature above our circumstances. Frame every experience through the lens of the truth of Jesus. Risk being different than the culture around us, perhaps even different than our own church cultures, by praying for the sick and making demonic oppressors leave in the Name of Jesus.

What's Next Activation

— *Prayer* —

Heavenly Father, I ask in the Name of Jesus that You give me the boldness and courage You gave to Joshua and Caleb, and yet teach me to come to You as a little child. Your Word says I am a new creation in You, and today I declare that is true! I pray that through the power of the Holy Spirit You give me ears to hear You, eyes to see You, and the ability trust You as my loving and protective Father. Help me to discern clearly what is from You, for You said that Your sheep hear Your voice. Thank You for giving me victory and setting things in advance for me to do according to Your will and Your glory. Peace and joy in the Holy Spirit are mine now and throughout every moment of my life. In Your Name and through Your authority and power. I am invited by You to do greater things than even You did. I am now, and forevermore, Yours and You are mine. Amen.

Give It Away

In your prayer time, ask the Holy Spirit who He would like for you to pray for today. Ask Him for revelation on what to say. You may only receive a simple thing or perhaps have an impression you are not certain about. Remember, you are bold and courageous, and when we give away Jesus' love, we are releasing His healing presence. You do not have to be profound to be germane. Childlike faith is simply deciding to try. Understand that you won't have all the answers, but you can trust our heavenly Father. He will use you to transform each life in front of you through simple kindness or extravagant miracles. Jesus and you are an unbeatable team, so practice putting on His love, healing power, and authority, and make yourself available. Even if you are shaking in your shoes, don't chicken out. The world needs Jesus, and you are His light.

4

The Power of Agreement

WE HAVE A TENTATIVE AGREEMENT,
WE DON'T EXPECT ANYTHING
TO BE CHANGED.

JEFF LUNGREN

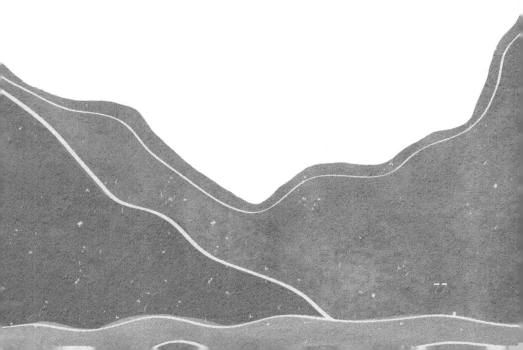

Pablo Battari was a minister who served under the great Argentinian evangelist Carlos Anacondia. He said, "Satan can't harm a believer's spirit, but he can harm their bodies, emotions and thoughts. The Lord uses our spirit to change our minds and sanctify our bodies, while Satan uses our bodies to ruin our minds and quench the spirit." Battari was the overseer for the healing tents in the Carlos Anacondia revival meetings during the 1980s, and he personally saw a hundred thousanad people set free from spiritual oppression. Since my own radical miracle healing, our Agape Freedom Fighter team has been privileged to pray for thousands of people and watch the love of Jesus Christ break them free from their agreement with the enemy's lies over their bodies, minds, and lives.

Agreement means to come into harmony with something. What we come into an agreement with we give power to. What we regularly consider and mull over in our mind is what brings about an expectancy for limitation or expectancy for improvement. What you think about matters more than you know. Until my own healing, I never realized how I had empowered the enemy's lies in my thoughts, my words, and my actions by simply agreeing with them.

When doubt and deception entered my mind, through my own thoughts or through the discouraging words of medical professionals, I rarely rejected them but allowed them to take root and gain ground in my life by agreeing with them. I resigned myself to the powerless position that God is sovereign, in control of everything, and therefore can do whatever He wants. He can heal anyone at any time if He wants to do that. That sounds even a tiny bit noble and honoring on the surface but, as these thoughts gained strength, I came to believe God must not be willing to heal me because He would be more glorified in my continued suffering than my healing.

Romans 8:17 says that if we share in His glory we will share in His sufferings. I thought God was teaching me a lesson through this pain and that physical sickness was part of the suffering I must do in order to inherit eternal life. But the word *sufferings* Paul used in Romans 8:17 actually refers to persecution and not physical illness. I had never been taught that truth. Instead, I adopted the thought that I must not be worthy to be healed because I am a sinner and sinners must suffer.

Wait a minute!

Christ died for my sins and took my frailties upon Himself on the cross. Paul reminds us in Second Timothy 1:6 that we are to fire up the gift of faith that is within us. Philippians 4:8 says that our meditation is to be on what is pure, noble, lovely, admirable, excellent, and praiseworthy. There it is again, what we consider in our mind is powerful. James 4:7 says that we are to resist the enemy and watch him flee. We do that by agreeing with the Word of God.

But I think this where the shortfall is—each of us starts looking for the pattern or formula of God for how long we have to wait or press in or all the other unknowns. God is mysterious, and yet we are to never stop praying and that's the hardest thing. Prayer becomes a rote and even a disconnected practice without the relationship of intimacy with the Lord. I have learned that above all else, we have a Father in Heaven who loves us and desires to be with us, a Savior and King who heals us and makes us whole, and a best Friend and Lover who moves mountains through our simple acts. The "make or break" position for every believer is that everything we need to stand against the trappings and sufferings of this world is found in intimacy with the Lord and a lifestyle of worship.

Worship as warfare is modeled throughout the Bible. Just before victory, the tribes of Israel worshiped. Jonah worshiped in the belly of the whale before he was barfed up on shore (although, I think most of us focus more on the barfing than the worship). In the New Testament, Paul and Silas worshiped from prison before they were freed (see Acts 16:25). All of this is about coming into agreement with the Word of God, as demonstrated through the exercise of our will, the activation of our faith, and participation in our own healing and freedom. Jonah, Paul, and Silas all chose to declare what is true with God before it actually took place. Worship is a way of professing with your mouth the truth of the Kingdom of Heaven, despite what you are currently experiencing or feeling. This is the power of agreement in action. Jesus said when the demons fled at His word, the Kingdom had come upon the people (see Luke 11:20). That remains true today.

Scripture says the power of life and death is in the tongue and we are to put away all evil talk (see Prov. 18:21; Eph. 4:31). For some of us, the evilest thoughts and language we have is against ourselves. The Word of God is alive and active, and the power of the Holy Spirit is within us. John 3:16 says God loved us so much that He sent Jesus and that by faith in Him we would not only have eternal life but freedom in this life. True victory in Jesus is found in the proclamation of the Word of God through prayer and through worship. When you feel weak, worship. When you feel defeated, declare what the Word of God says is true. I wish anyone had told me that when I was afflicted.

A few years ago, I had just flown home from Brazil when I received a text message from my friend Travis asking if I would join him to pray for a man named Steve whom he had recently met. I was extremely tired and with only a week before I left on my next ministry trip, my time at home was precious. My inclination was to say no to the request, but for the familiar hesitation I felt in my spirit. Seeking the will of the Lord in this matter, I felt a compelling impression that I was to go and pray for this man.

Two days later, at 8:00 a.m., I met Travis at a prayer room in the next city. He told me Steve was a well-known professional athlete who had endured a serious injury that had forced him into early retirement. He was about to be married, had recently become a Christian, and was desperate to be free from constant debilitating hip and back pain. My friend Travis was the photographer for his wedding and had watched him limping at the engagement photo shoot. Travis believes in miracles.

"You look like you're in pain," Travis had said to Steve at their first meeting.

"Yeah, it's always there. I've had five hip surgeries now and I can't play anymore. I had to retire." Steve shifted his weight and forced a smile.

"Can I pray for you? I believe Jesus heals today and I've seen Him do amazing things." Travis seizes any opportunity the Lord gives to him because he loves the adventure.

"Sure." Steve agreed to let Travis place his hands on his back and hip, and when Travis commanded all the pain to leave in the Name of Jesus, it did. Halleluiah! They were elated.

Several days later Steve texted Travis to thank him for praying, but the pain had returned. That's when Travis texted me.

I now stood face to chest with one of the tallest men I have ever seen. He seemed to be at least eight feet tall, but maybe it was more like six feet eight inches. He was soft-spoken, in his early thirties, with a huge smile and contagious enthusiasm for what Jesus was about to do, even though he had no idea what that would be. Steve had faith for healing despite his pain returning. He was blown away that Travis wanted to pray for him again and had invited me along. Being a brand-new Christian, Steve had no idea what was normal and what was not. Fantastic! What a God setup!

Travis always has faith for healing, and I am always thrilled to be part of whatever God has planned. Praying by formulas, or based on what happened yesterday, robs us of our ability to be dependent on God in the moment. The more dependent we are on the Holy Spirit for His direction throughout each day, the more glory God receives and the more bowled over we get to be at the creativity and extravagant love of the Father. Because the love of God is beyond our scope of understanding, I often read Romans 5:3-5 in *The Message* as a reminder of how I partner with God for each person He is desiring to touch no matter how troubling their lives and afflictions. Paul writes:

There's more to come: We continue to shout our praise even when we're hemmed in with troubles, because we know how troubles can develop passionate patience in us, and how that patience in turn forges the tempered steel of virtue, keeping us alert for whatever God will do next. In alert expectancy such as this, we're never left feeling shortchanged. Quite the contrary—we can't round up enough containers to hold everything God generously pours into our lives through the Holy Spirit!

The Holy Spirit always has a unique way of ministering to each person. I look to Him and wait. While I waited on Holy Spirit, I looked to Steve. I could feel the excitement of the Holy Spirit building as if to say, *Go ahead, it's time.* Sometimes praying for people is like that. There is a sense that the Lord has something wonderful planned, and we are invited to His party.

I almost burst out laughing as I glanced over at Travis, who was now grinning his infectious "This is going to be wild" smile. We stood in a circle in the middle of the prayer room. Couches lined the wall and chairs were set up at random. The lighting was dim for early morning, and the air-conditioning was running high.

"So, Steve, are you better standing or sitting?" I asked.

"It hurts either way so whatever works. I'm good with either."

I listened but was immediately distracted by the Holy Spirit as the Lord impressed upon me, *Sit down with him across from you. Ask him why he believes he is a disappointment. Don't pray for his hip yet.* It was just too weird of an impression to not be the Lord.

"Okay, Steve and Trav, let's sit here."

Steve sat on the couch in front of me.

Travis sat to my right, boiling over with enthusiasm and smiling brighter than the morning sunrise.

"Before we pray, I feel like the Lord wants me to ask you something. I could be totally wrong here. So, if I am, I apologize, and then we'll get on with praying."

Steve was staring at me, and Travis's smile was so wide, it touched his ears on either side. Travis knew.

"Why do you believe you're a disappointment, Steve?" I am used to the shocked look on a person's face when the Lord reveals the secrets of their heart, but I am always amazed at the way these secrets become the keys to unlock healing and destiny.

Tears filled Steve's eyes. The presence of the Holy Spirit thickened in the room.

"Steve, sometimes the things we believe about ourselves have a part to play in our healing. God's Word says that as a man thinks so he is.

Would you be okay if we pray for healing around this before we pray for your hip and back pain?

Steve nodded.

"Would you close your eyes?"

With eyes closed, Steve leaned into the back of the couch.

"Holy Spirit, thank You for being here. In the Name of Jesus, would You bring to Steve's mind the very first time he felt he was a disappointment?" We waited for less than a minute.

"I can't believe I'm thinking of this. Oh my gosh. That's crazy." Tears began to flow down Steve's face and drop onto his navy-blue shirt. "It's my dad. He's standing behind me and I'm looking up at him over my head. I think he's disappointed in me."

Travis began quietly interceding in prayer while we continued.

"How old are you here?" I asked.

"About five. I remember this like it was yesterday. His face looks like he's upset."

"Would you ask the Holy Spirit to show you where Jesus is in the room with you and your dad?"

"He's right here beside us. He's got His hand on my shoulder."

"Would you repeat after me a short prayer, Steve?"

"Yeah, sure."

"Lord Jesus, thank You that you are here. I choose to forgive my dad for making me feel like I am a disappointment to him."

As Steve was repeating this prayer, he began to cry harder.

"Tell me what's happening now, Steve."

"I am not a disappointment to my dad. I feel like Jesus is showing me my dad had a bunch of work things on his mind and the look on his face didn't have anything to do with me."

"Ask Jesus what is true about what your dad really thinks of you."

Now a stream of truth came forth, like the water bursting through a dam wall. "My dad is my biggest fan. He was my coach, my cheering squad, and the whole reason I ever was able to get into professional sports. He constantly encouraged me. Never raised his voice to me. He has never missed a game, even if he had to catch it on television because of his work schedule. My dad loves me."

The Word says that we shall know the truth and the truth shall set us free (see John 8:32). Steve was learning the truth. His chin quivered and raw emotion poured from his heart as the revelation of the Lord continued.

"Holy Spirit, please show Steve what other lies around disappointment he needs to break agreement with."

Steve didn't hesitate. "My coaches. All of my coaches. I have believed that I've been a disappointment to them...to the team...and even to my fiancé."

"How about to yourself?" I asked.

A loud sob escaped his lips. "I have been disappointed in myself my whole life."

"Now you have the ability, in Jesus, to get rid of these lies for good."

"Just tell me what to pray. I am ready." Steve choked.

"Please, repeat this: 'Father, in the Name of Jesus, I now choose to break every agreement with the enemy's lies that I am a disappointment to my father, my family, coaches, my fiancé, and even a disappointment to myself. I am not a disappointment. I am valuable, I am worthy, and I am loved. I command the spirit of rejection and fear to leave me now, in the Name of Jesus. Thank You, Holy Spirit for giving me divine revelation and thank You, Jesus, for filling me with Your love and truth.'"

"How are you feeling, Steve?" Travis asked.

Steve opened his eyes and smiled. "I feel like a ton of bricks came off me."

We laughed.

"Yep," I said. "We both know what that feels like, huh, Trav?"

I felt a nudge from the Holy Spirit to ask Steve to stand and check out his hip, even though we had not yet prayed for his physical healing. "Hey, stand up and check out your hip and back." We stood with him.

Steve began squatting up and down and kicking his legs out. "What?! No way! I don't have any pain! This is crazy!" He started jumping and running around the room while Travis and I laughed.

The three of us hugged and praised God. The Lord then gave me more words about Steve's sensitivity and passion to bring encouragement to others. I let him know this was not a weakness, but a gift, and one of the biggest reasons his fiancée fell in love with him. The Holy Spirit was encouraging this mighty man, in the most personal and unique way, as only God can do. Steve's eyes shone with God's love and the power of Jesus' healing touch.

"I don't get how you guys know all this stuff," Steve said. "I mean, I know God tells you, but wow, I want to do that!"

"We believe you will, Steve, because it's who you are, as the heir of Jesus Christ. He's got so much planned for your life."

"You know what? After all this, I sure don't think I need to be relegated to pharmaceutical sales. I thought that was the only thing I could do as a former professional athlete, because everyone else ends up doing it." We were listening to a free man—no longer bound by a limited, distorted view of his worth and destiny. That is the healing power of Jesus.

Steve and his fiancée married a few months later, and Travis photographed their wedding. As Travis tells it, it was an amazing day. Steve remained free from pain, and although we haven't seen him lately, I am sure he is doing what he loves while passionately pursuing intimacy with God. Whom the Son sets free is indeed free (see John 8:36). Steve is now living what Psalm 34 describes.

I bless God every chance I get; my lungs expand with his praise. I live and breathe God; if things aren't going well, hear this and be happy: Join me in spreading the news; together let's get the word out. God met me more than half-way, he freed me from my anxious fears. Look at him; give him your warmest smile. Never hide your feelings from him. When I was desperate, I called out, and God got me out of a tight spot. God's angel sets up a circle of protection around us while we pray. Open your mouth and taste, open your eyes and see—how good God is. Blessed are you who run to him. Worship God if you want the best; worship opens doors to all his goodness (verses 1-9 MSG).

Steve had a mindset of disappointment and self-deprecation for most of his life. When he suffered his first injury, it further reinforced his thoughts that if he had been faster, more agile, or stronger he would not have been injured. One lie begat another, and eventually his mindset was permeated with the thought that no matter what he did, he would never measure up. In one brief meeting with Jesus, all of the lies were exposed, and the truth of how loved, accepted, and powerful Steve really is in Christ was made known to him. Now he is on the journey as each of us is—to live actively aware of the lies of the enemy and to break our agreement with them. And in the same breath, to invite the Holy Spirit to show us again who we really are.

What's Next Activation

Sit quietly and play instrumental worship music if it helps you relax. In a position of rest, without striving, simply thank the Lord for bringing healing to every area of your life—your mind, physical body, and soul. Close your eyes and take a few relaxed breaths. Pray, "Holy Spirit, show me what lies I have believed about how others view me or what I believe about myself, because others have caused me to feel rejected or disapproved of."

Focus your attention on Jesus, in a posture of receiving. God promises you will find Him when you seek Him with all of your heart (see Jer. 29:13). The Holy Spirit may bring you back to a memory. With that memory in mind, ask, "Jesus, what is the lie I believe about this situation, memory, or person?"

Wait for the Lord to give you an impression, a thought, or a clear word. Once you have the lie clarified, ask Jesus what the truth is. Keep your eyes closed while you listen, watch, and think. All of us receive messages from the Holy Spirit in different ways. Some think more than see, some hear more than think, but all of our senses and imagination are sanctified in Christ. Once you know the truth, you have the opportunity break agreement with the lie and to empower the truth. Whatever we agree with, we empower. When we empower a lie, that becomes our reality. It is now time to take back those areas and allow Jesus to bring freedom.

— *Prayer* —

Lord, thank You for showing me the truth. I break my agreement with the lie that I am _____.
That is not true. I am free in You, Jesus. I am loved, accepted, and valued. I now sever any tie with this lie and tell any oppressive spirit attached to it to leave in the Name of Jesus Christ. Holy Spirit, come and fill me up completely with Your perfect love, joy, and peace. Thank You, Jesus.

Give It Away

In Matthew 10:7-8, Jesus told the disciples they had freely been given His power and authority through the Holy Spirit to do what He did. They were to freely give it away. His instructions for the disciples are also for us. God isn't waiting for you to get everything right. He is simply inviting you to partner with Him and practice loving people in front of you. Today, look for the prompting of the Lord to pray for someone as you have just prayed for yourself. I promise you, the Lord is faithful in our weakest attempts to simply give away His compassion.

NOTE

1. Pablo Battari, *Free in Christ* (Lake Mary, FL: Charisma House, 2000).

5

The Key of Forgiveness

TO FORGIVE IS TO SET A PRISONER
FREE AND TO DISCOVER THAT
PRISONER WAS YOU.

LEWIS B. SMEDES

Scripture after Scripture speaks of the importance of our willingness to forgive those who have offended or hurt us. Matthew 6:14-15 (NIV) says, *"For if you forgive other people when they sin against you, your heavenly Father will also forgive you. But if you do not forgive others their sins, your Father will not forgive your sins."* Colossians 3:13 (NIV) says, *"Bear with each other and forgive one another if any of you has a grievance against someone. Forgive as the Lord forgave you."* And First Corinthians 13:4-6 speaks of love being patient and kind, without envy or boast, void of arrogance or resentment, and without rejoicing at wrongdoing.

I knew the power of forgiveness firsthand because of my own healing. I realized the power of forgiving oneself as well, but I will admit that initially I had not yet reasoned that Jesus meant forgive *all* offenses. After all, I had succumbed to what most of us do—to place sin into categories. The first category was a list of sins that I believed was acceptable to forgive while the other was a litany of sins I believed could not be pardoned. For example, for many years, I thought, the more atrocious the abuse was against innocent children, the less pardonable that type of sin would be. Because of my personality and my desire to see justice prevail, I have had a very difficult time with the concept of forgiveness for every and all offense according to God's standard. My problem is that I created my own standard of judgment. I had not yet fully understood what forgiveness truly is or, more importantly, how vast God's forgiveness is toward every human being. I am learning.

Today, I understand forgiveness is first and foremost simply admitting that an offense has been committed.[1] I remember how relieved I was when I finally learned the truth. Maybe as you read this, you are too. In moments of forgiveness, a deep need to be vindicated would always rise up and choke me, but as soon as I discovered God's standard and His desire to give each of His children a voice to express the injustice done to us, the internal pressure-cooker valve of my soul whistled a shrill warning and the compression of injustice escaped through grace. God's standard for forgiveness is to first admit the offense happened. When we do this, denial will no longer be part of the enemy's plan to silence us and cause the internal pressure to remain cranked on high. Thank God. Denial looks rather noble to some on the outside when in reality, the enemy has a field day with us stuffing our hurt and resentment on the inside. We won't allow Jesus to restore freedom until we admit the struggle is there. This is important for those who have felt forced to forget an incident or abuse—either because your family refused to acknowledge it, or the shame of revealing it has been too overwhelming. Forgiveness through Jesus Christ removes the *power* of the painful memory over your life.

Forgiveness never declares what the offenders did is acceptable, nor does it conceal the seriousness of the hurt or offense. Forgiveness isn't saying you aren't owed something. Catherine Marshall, in her book *Something More*, describes forgiveness as releasing another person from our personal judgment.[2] In other words, we are taking a person from our personal judgment and without agreeing with what they've done, we no longer stand in the place as their judge. Jesus described forgiveness as the releasing of a debt in Matthew 6:12 (NIV): "*And forgive us our debts, as we also have forgiven our debtors.*" A debt is something owed to us.[3]

Forgiveness also means we release our offenders from the debt and the punishment we believe they deserve. Some of us believe our abusers and offenders deserve to suffer as we have suffered. One thing I have learned while traveling and praying for thousands of people over the years is most abusers have suffered the same abuse they have inflicted on others. It tends to be a vicious cycle. The enemy seeks to destroy and kill the children of God. There is a force of darkness in the demonic that is attached to people and families when cycles of abuse through generations exist. These are destined to be repeated unless we choose Jesus. We are powerless to change without Christ, but with Him everything is possible (see Matt. 19:26).

Forgiveness acknowledges the debt, but we actively choose to cancel it. When we cancel the debt, the bondage through the offense against us is removed and, in turn, the attachment to the offender and the offense is removed. My friend Kelsey describes the act of forgiveness as cutting loose the anchor that tethers us. I love this prophetic picture. Cancelling debt releases the offender to the Just judge and our Defender, Jesus Christ, and sets us free. The Word of God is clear: *"Never take your own revenge, beloved, but leave room for the wrath of God, for it is written, 'Vengeance is Mine, I will repay,' says the Lord"* (Romans 12:19 NASB). Holding the offense puts us smack in God's way. When we refuse to forgive and hold on tight to the offense, we remove the ability for Jesus to take control of the healing process and God to render His justice. God cannot be judge if we stand between Him and our offender. To choose to forgive is not setting our offenders free. It is the choice to set ourselves free and trust that Jesus Christ is the Person of Truth and our Lord has more than just our healing within His love. He also has our destiny. We cannot sail with Him into the future if we are anchored in our past hurt, fear, and unforgiveness.

Another focus about the process of forgiveness is that our willingness to forgive cannot be dependent upon the actions and choices of our offender; rather, it is dependent on us choosing to release the debt and be free from bitterness, judgment, and anger.[4] Forgiveness releases our assumptions and expectations, even if they are legitimate. It acknowledges the expectation and lets it go.[5]

Forgiveness does not mean we have to invite the offender into relationship with us. Forgiveness begins first and foremost between each individual and the Lord. Forgiveness does not mean we let go of our boundaries and make ourselves vulnerable for further abuse. Boundaries are often necessary. Trust has to be earned and rebuilt.

Choosing to forgive doesn't mean we instantly feel better. Forgiveness is not a feeling; it is a decision. We don't forgive with our emotions. We forgive with our will. I asked God many questions concerning forgiveness and childhood abuse. In one particular instance, when I was praying for a young woman who had tragically experienced years of torment throughout her childhood, I asked the Lord why He didn't stop the abuse. I felt the Holy Spirit impress on me that God would not violate the free will of her abuser. Because to remove free will for one is to remove free will for all. Although that was hard for me to understand at the time, I now understand more fully since God does not show favoritism (see Acts 10:34).

He is clear throughout Scripture that there is a way to stop committing atrocities against one another. Isaiah 55:6-7 (NIV) says, *"Seek the Lord while he may be found; call on him while he is near. Let the wicked forsake their ways and the unrighteous their thoughts. Let them turn to the Lord, and he will have mercy on them and to our God, for he will freely pardon."* Galatians 5:13 (NIV) says, *"You, my brothers and sisters, were called to be free. But do not use your freedom to indulge the flesh; rather, service one another humbly in love."* And finally, from First Corinthians 10:13 (NIV): *"No temptation has overtaken you except what is common to mankind. And God is faithful; he will not let you be tempted beyond what you can beat. But when you are tempted, he will also provide a way out so that you can endure it."*

Just as God will not violate the free will of the offender, He also will not violate our free will to forgive our abuser or defiler either. It is up to us to choose.

Once, while teaching at a conference, I noticed a small, lovely, dark-haired woman of about fifty years old hanging out against one of the doorjambs for much of the day. Her eyes darted around the room, and she shifted her weight side to side. I glanced over at her, occasionally feeling the compassion of Jesus for this anxious daughter of God. She was clearly nervous and ready to bolt at any moment. I remarked to the Lord to help me connect with her later and asked the Holy Spirit to cover her with peace.

The next morning, she was back at the doorway again, and our Agape ministry team was praying over people while worship was happening. I walked over to her and asked her name.

"I'm Anna," she replied while avoiding all eye contact.

"I'm happy to meet you, Anna. Are you okay?"

"I just don't understand any of this. I go to church, but this is not like my church, and my sister wanted me to come with her."

"I'm glad you're here." As I spoke the words, I received a word of knowledge about back and hip pain. "Anna, I am wondering if you have back and hip pain?"

She audibly sucked in air and looked up at me with wild eyes. "I've had back and hip pain, unbearable pain, all of my life because I was born with scoliosis. I have..." Her voice trailed away, and she pointed to her left foot. She wore a sandal built up with more than five inches of height on her left leg only. Her right foot was encased in a matching flat sandal.

I looked into her eyes, now spilling over with tears. Through the presence of the Holy Spirit and the love of Jesus, I saw a lifetime of abuse, cruelty, rejection, and abandonment in her eyes. My heart was overwhelmed with love for this woman. "Would it be okay if I hugged you?"

Anna responded with a nod while the tears flowed.

As I hugged her, I saw two very vivid visions of violent childhood abuse. But I remained focused on Jesus because I know the power of words of knowledge to bring healing to people. I also know firsthand the promise of Romans 8:28: *"God causes everything to work together for the good of those who love God and are called according to his purpose for them."* I felt the gift of faith rise within me through the power of the Holy Spirit. Like David in the Scriptures, I have seen the goodness of the Lord in the land of the living so many times and His mighty miracle-working power in more than just my own healing, so I was excited about what was about to happen. I asked the Holy Spirit for her age at the time of each of the incidents.

"Seven and nine years old," I heard.

After asking the Lord for wisdom, I felt led to whisper in her ear, "What happened to you when you were age seven and age nine in Guatemala was not your fault. What those two men did to you was wrong. You have never told anyone because of their threats against you."

Then the dam burst. Anna fell forward farther into my embrace and wailed. I held her while her body heaved with emotion, and others began looking at us because of the noise. Anna's sister came over at that moment—already in tears. She knew from the Lord what was about to happen and began quietly interceding a few feet away from us.

"Jesus wants to help you," I said. "Would it be okay if I pray for you?"

Anna tried to nod but only cried harder.

I held her and whispered in her ear, "Would you look at me for a moment?" Anna picked her head up, and I invited the presence of the Holy Spirit to cover her in perfect peace. "None of it was your fault," I repeated as she looked into my eyes.

This time she tried to hold my gaze. Over the next five minutes we engaged in prayer. I asked her to first imagine Jesus in front of her as her Protector. She said she could feel His presence.

I asked if she would also imagine her abusers behind Jesus, then, "Is Jesus a safe person for you and are you okay to continue?"

Anna nodded in response.

"Would you let Jesus know how you felt about what happened to you? Would you speak whatever you feel you never had the chance to say to those who hurt you? Direct those words to Jesus as your Covering and Protector. These men can never harm you again. Okay?"

Anna nodded again and closed her eyes to focus on Jesus.

The power of the Holy Spirit was very evident on Anna, and others a few feet away from Anna's sister were now interceding as well.

Anna spoke softly. "Jesus, what those men did to me was wrong." Fresh tears began to flow. "I was so small, and no matter what they said to me, it wasn't my fault and I didn't deserve it. They hurt me, Jesus, and I have been so afraid since then."

With tears covering her face, I quietly leaned into her ear and encouraged her. I briefly explained what forgiveness really means and asked if she would be willing to engage in forgiving her abusers.

She said that she would. With simple childlike faith she forgave each one—even asking God to deal with the men in mercy.

"How are you feeling right now?" I asked.

"I don't know what's happening! I feel like a very heavy weight is no longer on me."

"Will you repeat this prayer after me?" I was smiling now. "Lord, I forgive my parents for not protecting me, and I break every agreement that I will always be unprotected and afraid. I am not rejected or abandoned. I am not unlovable. I am loved by Jesus."

As Anna spoke these words, the power of the Holy Spirit came upon her with such weight that she fell down and went out under the glory and power of God. Twice she tried to sit up and yelled, "I can see angels!"

Her sister was laughing and crying at the same time. So was I.

I was crying at the goodness of almighty God to encounter each of His children exactly as they have need.

What came next, I could not imagine.

Anna eventually sat up. Still very shaky and not able to comprehend what happened.

"How is your back and hip pain?" I asked. Slowly, her sister and I lifted her from the ground, so she could move around.

She began to laugh. "I don't have any!"

"That's right. But now the Lord wants us to pray for your spine to straighten and your legs to be exactly the same length."

Anna was too under the power of the Holy Spirit to protest anything. We sat her in a chair and prayed for her spine to straighten in the Name of Jesus. Visibly, we watched her spine straighten. Next, we took Anna's legs and in the mighty Name of Jesus, commanded the legs to align perfectly.

"Anna, what do you see?"

"What? My legs are the same! What?" Her sister and friend walked her around the room while she yelled, "Thank You, Jesus!" over and over again.

I stood marveling again at the incredible love of God. Gratitude filled my heart as I approached the platform to teach the first morning session.

That evening, Anna came into the service, approached me, and said, "These are my sister's sandals because none of my shoes work anymore."

I hugged and hugged her and saw what I never get tired of seeing. True freedom in a child of God.

There is no better life.

Over the years I have heard from many clergy that true forgiveness only occurs when there is reconciliation between both parties. But because the very definition of reconciliation means to bring harmony, agreement, and the restoration of friendly relations—the position of these well-meaning clergy cannot stand as a true proof of forgiveness. Forgiveness doesn't mean reconciliation is the next step or is the primary objective because reconciliation insists that both parties seek harmony, friendly relations, and the desire to work through a restoration process. If only one half of the party desires restoration while the other doesn't, this does not mean forgiveness did not occur. Forgiveness focuses on addressing the offense, while reconciliation focuses on the relationship. As I clarified earlier, forgiveness takes place between us and God through the person of Jesus Christ.

If we are led to reconcile, asking for the wisdom of the Holy Spirit for timing and personal motivation is critical. The Bible is clear in Matthew 18:15-17 to go first to the person in private. But, if the person has never repented and has a history of being unsafe, it is always best to seek wise godly council before connecting with the person. Reconciliation can be a work in progress, while still maintaining appropriate boundaries to prevent further wounding.

In Anna's case, due to the nature of the relationship with the family members who abused her, Anna did not feel reconciliation was possible. She let me know that the sexual abuse of young girls is common and therefore would not be recognized by these men or her family as being that important. I was heartbroken to hear the news, but I know that according to First Timothy 2:4, God desires all men to be saved and to come to the knowledge of the truth. So, until they have another leading from the Lord, Anna and her sister continue to pray for their whole family, just as each of us are called to do for our own. Prayer changes everything.

What's Next Activation

Every family has issues. No one has escaped without some level of hurt and pain. Maybe you have already dealt with your major forgiveness issues, and that is wonderful. I have discovered even when I feel surrendered to the Lord and believe I'm doing well, it is worth asking the Lord for His perspective. Most days, I invite the Lord to examine my motivation and the health of my relationships. There are always places the Holy Spirit desires to heal, and some of that requires me to become aware of an offense I have stuffed deep down because I am busy or wanted to avoid conflict. Often, I am made aware that I did not treat someone with the loving-kindness of Jesus. Sometimes, that someone I did not treat with the loving-kindness of Jesus is me. Forgiveness is applicable to all of your relationships, including the care of yourself. Right now, let's stop together and pray.

> *Lord, I invite You to bring any areas of offense or misunderstanding that You desire to be addressed. If I have unforgiveness toward anyone—even myself—please show me now in the Name of Jesus.*

— *Forgiveness Prayer for Another Person* —

In the Name of Jesus, I choose to forgive because Your Word says You forgave me first. I choose to forgive _____. I no longer retain my right to judge, condemn, or seek revenge against them. Through forgiveness and the release of their offense against me, I no longer give them any right to cause me intimidation and fear. Any debt they owe to me is now cancelled, and I break any harmful words I have spoken about them. I turn them over to You, Lord Jesus, and ask that You grant them mercy, as You have shown me mercy, and bless their lives and families. Thank You for the grace to forgive and the power to live in freedom.

— *Forgiveness Prayer for Yourself* —

Father, in the Name of Jesus, I choose to forgive myself. I will no longer judge and condemn myself but trust that You have made me a new creation in You. I break my agreement with perfectionism and comparison. You do not condemn me, so I will no longer condemn myself. You restored me onto the lap of my heavenly Father and gave me Your righteousness and likeness as a child of God and co-heir with You. Thank You for my life. I cut off the right of the demonic to afflict me because of self-rejection

*and unworthiness. I break every assignment of dark-
ness against me by the power of Your Name, Jesus, and
command all unclean spirits to leave now. I receive the
fullness of Your love and acceptance. Come, Holy Spirit,
and fill me with the Father's love and the fullness of joy
in You.*

Give It Away

Forgiveness as a way of life takes practice. As you go through each day, ask the Holy Spirit to give you a quick convicting nudge when you create a judgment about someone or adopt any part of unforgiveness. Ask Him what to do in response. Often, the Holy Spirit will invite me to release kindness and love over the one who just offended me. It's like having a large callus on the side of your foot shaved off. It isn't pleasant but when it is finished, we are not so rough around the edges.

NOTES

1. Rodney Hogue, *Forgiveness* (Collierville, TN: Instant Publisher, 2008).

2. Catherine Marshall, *Something More* (Harper Collins, 1994).

3. Hogue, *Forgiveness*.

4. Hogue, *Forgiveness*.

5. Hogue, *Forgiveness*.

6

Love as I Love You

IF I WERE TO SPEAK WITH ELOQUENCE IN EARTH'S
MANY LANGUAGES AND IN HEAVENLY TONGUES OF
ANGELS YET I DIDN'T EXPRESS MYSELF WITH LOVE,
MY WORDS WOULD BE REDUCED TO THE HOLLOW SOUND
OF NOTHING MORE THAN A CLANGING SYMBOL. AND
IF I WERE TO HAVE THE GIFT OF PROPHECY WITH A
PROFOUND UNDERSTANDING OF GOD'S HIDDEN SECRETS
AND IF I POSSESSED UNENDING SUPERNATURAL
KNOWLEDGE, AND IF I HAD THE GREATEST GIFT OF
FAITH THAT COULD MOVE MOUNTAINS BUT HAVE NEVER
LEARNED TO LOVE THAN I AM NOTHING.

1 CORINTHIANS 13:1-2 TPT

I have come to understand that we have to practice putting on love. I have a dear friend who does this all day long. She is a public high school teacher in a school of more than 4,000 with an extremely diverse student body. I believe it's safe to say there are probably more than 10 native languages common to the students there. I've prayed for several of their parents, and none of them spoke English. Many of these families live in poverty and brokenness. Instead of seeing challenges and obstacles here, my friend Sarah sees gold. More than a decade ago, the Lord gave Sarah an idea on how to bring healing and transformation, not only to her own students but the student body at large, their families, community, and city. Sarah dreams big with God, and He answers her.

With student leadership and Sarah as the faculty advisor, Breakthrough was formed. Breakthrough is an afterschool Christian club geared to teach the Word of God, host the presence of the Holy Spirit, train all students to hear the voice of God, and move in the healing love of Jesus to all of those around them. The Bible says signs, wonders and miracles will follow all who believe. Sarah knows there is no lack when it comes to the Lord's gifts. She also knows that the intrinsic value of every person is found in God. Mankind is of incalculable worth to God because of the price paid for our redemption. *"For ye were bought with a price: therefore glorify God in your body, and in your spirit, which are God's"* (1 Corinthians 6:20 KJV).

Because Sarah sees the incalculable worth of every student walking through the halls, she became a celebrator of each of them—no matter where they are in the journey. First Corinthians 13:6-7 (TPT) says, *"Love joyfully celebrates honesty and finds no delight in what is wrong. Love is a safe place of shelter for it never stops believing the best for others."* This Scripture is the backbone for prophecy. Believing the best for someone who is strung out on drugs or failing in every class. That is what my friend Sarah does. She doesn't judge a student as they stand before her reeking of weed or alcohol. She hugs them and tells them she loves them. Sarah prophetically asks the Lord for His heart of love for their lost souls and invites them to Breakthrough. When these students come after school to find out more about Breakthrough, they encounter an avalanche of love and acceptance from the other students who make up Breakthrough's student leadership.

For over a year, I had been hearing about the radical healings and salvations of whole families because of the tangible love of Jesus flowing out of Sarah and the students she was raising up. I was fascinated that in a United States public high school where prayer is banned, my friend is able to do healing ministry throughout the week despite the cameras mounted throughout the campus. On a spring day a few years ago, I flew to meet Sarah at her school and speak to the students at Breakthrough. I wanted to pray for these kids and watch Jesus bring healing transformation to their lives.

Once I arrived at the school, I had to come through a security metal detector and have the head of security register me.

"Hi, I'm Joanne Moody."

"I know who you are," said the woman in the cherry-red track suit. "Miss Thompson put up your posters all over this place."

Beside me, Sarah burst into laughter. "Hey, Helen, you weren't supposed to tell her that. It's a surprise!"

"What?" I laughed. "Posters?"

"Trust me, the kids think you are a celebrity, so they will all want to come to Breakthrough this afternoon."

All I could do was stare at her while the security guard stared at me.

"Helen, you should get Jo to pray for your knee."

Helen's eyes got twice the size. "Naw, I'm okay, Miss Thompson."

"What's the matter with your knee, Helen?"

"I blew out my ACL, and I can't get up the stairs. I have to use the elevator with my crutches."

"Sounds painful. I'd love to pray for you."

At my reply, Sarah was about to jump over the desk and pull Helen out. "Come on, Helen. There's a place upstairs. I promise it'll be worth your time."

Off the three of us went into the elevator and then into a small copy room.

"There aren't any cameras in here," Sarah said.

Helen looked like she wondered what she had agreed to.

I smiled. "Ready, Helen?"

"What do I do?" she asked.

"Just receive what Jesus wants to do," I said. "Tell me on a scale of one to ten if ten is the highest level of pain, what level do you have right now?"

"It's like a seven. Pretty bad. Hurts all the time and I can't move it very well or put my weight on it."

"Holy Spirit, thank You that You are here now. Father, in the Name of Jesus I command the ACL to be knit completely together and all pain to go in the Name of Jesus Christ."

"I feel heat on me! What is going on?!"

"Check out your knee, Helen. Try something you couldn't do before."

Helen squatted up and down and moved her knee completely normally. "This is just crazy! I don't have any pain! Come on!"

"Just say, 'Thank You, Jesus, for healing me!'"

"Thank You, Jesus!" Her face was having a dance party while her legs continued to try kicking, lunging, and squatting.

I laughed while Sarah was guffawing in the corner.

Helen put her hands to her face. "What? My nose, my throat! I had a sinus thing going on and it's gone too! I'm telling you what! Jesus is King, He sure is! That's right!"

We hugged all around and watched Helen jog down the stairs while we headed for the hallway before the bell rang for the next change of classes.

"This is fantastic!" I said to Sarah.

"You haven't even seen anything yet."

She took my arm and led me up another flight of stairs and down several hallways. The campus was huge.

"Okay," Sarah said. "Stand here with me when the bell rings. I'm looking for Alexa because I want you to pray for her. I'm not telling you anything about her."

"Fun!" I said as the bell sounded throughout the buildings and students of every size, shape, and color filled the hallways like salmon swimming upstream in both directions. I saw Sarah lift up on her toes to peer over the crowd, making a dash to her left and stepping in front of a petite dark-haired girl.

She motioned me over. "Hey, Alexa, this is my friend Jo."

Alexa lifted her chin in greeting but her face remained a mold of hopelessness and mistrust.

"Hey, Alexa, I'm glad to meet you." I felt the love of Jesus for this young woman.

"So, where's your next class, Alexa?" Sarah asked.

"Um, Mrs. Kirby, you know, 308."

"I'll be stopping by to take you out of that class a little early. Okay with you?" Alexa shrugged as Sarah hugged her. For a nanosecond, peace came over Alexa's face before the stone wall returned.

With a substitute handling her own class, Sarah and I headed back to the ground floor so I could pray for the school culinary arts teacher suffering from chronic neck pain. It was comical how quickly the Holy Spirit swept in to bring healing. The Lord knew how Sarah rolled. Limited access and limited time.

Let's move, Lord, and bring the light to as many as possible!

Back upstairs we climbed.

"You know, Alexa gave her life to Jesus a few weeks ago, but she's on a roller coaster ride," Sarah said over her shoulder. "I'm not going to tell you anything else." Then she moved down the hall and turned right to get Alexa out early from her last class of the day.

While I was waiting in the corridor, the custodian came by with her cart, and I received a word of knowledge to ask about a recent family loss. She began to cry and—overwhelmed with the Lord's love and desire to bring comfort to His child in mourning—I prayed for her broken heart. She hugged me, and I hugged her back when Sarah walked up smiling with Alexa.

"Let's go to my office." Sarah said.

Alexa and I followed her right into the school elevator.

No cameras here. Sarah mouthed the words to me, so Alexa didn't hear.

I was incredulous.

As the elevator doors closed, Sarah said, "Lord, I pray nobody presses the button for this elevator while we need it. In Jesus' Name. That will do it." She turned to Alexa. "Okay if Jo prays for you?"

"Yeah, I guess so."

While Alexa responded, I asked the Lord what was going on with her. I sensed she had a very painful lower back. "Do you have lower back pain?"

"Huh, what? Yeah! How do you know that?"

"Sometimes, God tells me stuff. This is because He loves you, and He doesn't want you to be in pain anymore." As soon as the words left my mouth, I felt that this young woman had been abused and abandoned by her father more than once.

The word of knowledge was fleeting while the overwhelming love of Jesus increased.

I continued, "You know, Alexa, when we forgive someone, it's a choice, not a feeling. It also doesn't make what the person did to us right. What your father did to you was wrong, but Jesus wants to know if you are willing to make the choice to forgive your father." Tears welled in her beautiful chocolate-brown eyes and spilled down her cheeks.

"How do you know that stuff?"

"I told you, honey. Jesus loves you, and He is telling me this, so you can be free."

Through her tears, Alexa prayed with me to forgive her father. I asked her to say that the abuse was not her fault in order to break the powerful curse words she had received most of her life. As she spoke these words, she cried out, "I don't know what is happening right now, but I can't feel my legs! Are my legs still on the ground? What? I feel like I'm floating. My legs are all tingly."

Sarah was in tears, and so was I. "Don't worry. This is just the presence of God. He loves you so much. Your legs are on the ground, yes. How is your back pain?"

"I don't have any back pain!" Alexa cried, shaking her head back and forth in disbelief. "You don't get it! I've had that pain for years, and it never goes away!"

I looked in to the eyes of this beautiful daughter of God and said, "Alexa, when you chose to forgive your father in the Name of Jesus, the forces of darkness no longer could hang on to your back. It's Jesus who healed you."

"I don't even know what to say."

"Just say, 'Thanks, Jesus.'"

"Thank You, Jesus," Alexa said just above a whisper.

"Is it okay if I hug you?"

The nod was all I needed.

As I pulled her close to me as a mother would hug a daughter, I spoke about her value to God. I told her that the person she was involved with was toxic, and she needed to believe she was priceless and pray to have the courage to be finished with the relationship she was in. The final bell sounded, and we rode the elevator to the floor where Sarah's classroom was and home to the Breakthrough gathering in fifteen minutes. Alexa wandered away to her locker with no back pain and a look of serenity on her face. Her entire countenance had shifted.

While we had been busy in the elevator, Helen, once skeptical about any reported healings that happened through Breakthrough, was now on fire for Jesus. She directed every student, staff, and faculty member to go to the Breakthrough meeting. She even called her mother to tell her she would be picking her up to bring her back to "get her own healing."

That's what Jesus does: Miracles through love. Healings when someone doesn't even know what's happening.

Since God sees every human life in our entirety, what better way to love people than to see them as God's finished perfection? We see people for who they are in Jesus—not as they stand before us. In the love of Jesus, we are all unblemished, forgiven, and cleansed. The Holy Spirit gives us the ability to see others as Jesus sees them. Only through the Father's love can we be a shelter for another—a shelter of love, healing, and freedom. We have the power to transform culture through simple acts of loving-kindness and generosity, by believing the best about each person.

That's what my friend Sarah does all day every day. During the summer months she goes into the women's prisons in her area and does the same thing she does in her school. This is what we are all called to do. We are called to be the healing love and freedom of Jesus. We'll never do everything perfectly—we simply need to say yes.

What's Next Activation

— Prayer —

Father, I admit that I have placed people in categories of acceptable and not acceptable, important, and easily forgotten. I've even labeled some crimes people commit or behavior they engage in as unforgiveable. Lord, please forgive me. I long to have the eyes that You have to see people as valuable, priceless treasures. I want to love as You love. No matter what any of us have done, You have paid the price, Jesus, for all to be saved, healed, and freed forever. I ask for more of Your love, Father. Love overflowing like a river that I give away what You have freely given to me. Set a fire in my soul and a passion for the lost. Make me bold and fearless so I become the catalyst of change for an entire region. When people meet me, may they know that I live for You and bring Your Name honor and glory. Thank You, Lord, that my name is written in the Lamb's book of life. Let me part-ner with You so that others may know eternity with You. In the Name of Jesus Christ, amen.

Give It Away

Without being religious, what will you partner with God to do this week that will allow others to see that their eternity is with Jesus Christ? Ask the Holy Spirit to give you something unique and creative. Breathe deeply, imagine, or think about Jesus being right next to you and do what the Holy Spirit showed or prompted you with. Some people have vivid imaginations while others think of ideas with God. Not one way is better than the other. We all experience God in a unique way. Allow the Holy Spirit to teach you the way He speaks to you.

7

The Truth about Trials

A DIAMOND IS MERELY A LUMP OF COAL
THAT DID WELL UNDER PRESSURE.

ANONYMOUS

For the fourteen and a half years of my physical suffering with nerve damage, I could not see the forest through the trees. I was deceived. I thought the suffering I was undergoing was producing a worthiness in me that would render me acceptable to God the Father. And that was only one of the lies I believed.

Maybe you have never been this confused or gullible, but I'll admit it, I have. I have met thousands of others who believe in Jesus and they are as misled as I was. I suspect some of us miss the all-encompassing truth of the gift of salvation and abundant life in Christ through a myriad of ways, but the most common reason is a lack of comprehension of the vastness of God's love for each and every person. I've noticed over the years as it pertains to human suffering that the enemy is not uniquely clever. He uses the same types of enticements and hooks on the sons and daughters of God. Make no mistake, the enemy of our souls is vigilant about our destruction. The Word of God says he prowls around like a roaring lion looking for anyone he can devour (see 1 Pet. 5:8). Yet, when we understand his ploys and pitfalls, we are less likely to trip into his snare.

First Corinthians 13:13 (ESV) says, *"So now faith, hope, and love abide, these three; but the greatest of these is love."* One of the common schemes of the enemy when we encounter difficulty, trial, and suffering is to convince us that God does not love us enough to deliver us from whatever mountain is crushing us. The enemy loves to plant ideas in our mind that we have been forgotten by God.

When my mom contracted MRSA in her finger, I asked if she wanted me to pray for her on the phone.

"Joanne, God has a whole lot of other people who need help more than I do, so that's okay."

What? My mom was duped. She believed that God is not large enough to bring healing to all of the sick ones—only to the *really* sick ones because, somewhere along the way we have made God human.

We reduce His love and faithfulness to levels of priority that we can understand. Romans 11:33 (TPT) says, *"Who, could ever wrap their minds around the riches of God, the depth of his wisdom, and the marvel of his perfect knowledge? Who could ever explain the wonder of his decisions or search out the mysterious way he carries out his plans?"* Yet, the Lord told Jeremiah that he would find the Lord if he searched with all of his heart (see Jer. 29:13).

In the search to understand, we will surely discover the inexhaustible love and acceptance from God our Father through Jesus Christ if we do not give up and do not give into fear. No wonder the enemy will do anything to distract us and cause us to believe we have been abandoned. Without love it is impossible to find authentic hope and the absence of hope leaves us void of faith. And without faith, we are powerless. Even the apostle Paul spoke of running the race until the end and keeping the faith. I am pretty sure after beatings, imprisonment, starvation, and shipwrecks, Paul knew how important intimacy with God was in order to grab hold of faith with all that was within him. In the midst of trouble, it is common to forget that we are to live by faith and not by sight (see 2 Cor. 5:7). But none of us can just muster up faith. Genuine faith is the fruit of divine love. Here we are again. Intimacy with Jesus is paramount for overcoming every trial, sickness, and tragedy to befall humankind.

It was a Tuesday morning, and several members of our Agape Freedom Fighters ministry team and I were headed back to the airport after two weeks of doing ministry in Europe. I had an overwhelming sense of the presence of the Holy Spirit in the dark hours before dawn. *Thank You, Holy Spirit, for Your presence. If there is anyone You desire for me*

to pray for at the airport, please show me. I threw the rest of my clothes in my bulging suitcase, hoofed it down three flights of stairs, and got into one of the two cars dropping us off curbside at the airport. I was contemplative, still feeling the presence of the Lord but not trying to be particularly holy. Laughter broke out as we spoke with our driving host of the great exploits of the Lord throughout our time together.

As I approached the terminal, I turned to Kathy, one of our team members. "I told the Lord I would stop and pray for anyone He wanted."

Kathy's face lit up as laughter burst from her lips like a song. "Okay, I'm in!" Her response was pure joy. I love Kathy's laugh when she knows the Lord is inviting us to something. "This is going to be good, Jo. I can just feel it."

I have been with Kathy on so many mission trips, and her gift of faith is palpable. Once she told me not to board our plane from Brazil because she was going to get a first-class upgrade.

"Kathy, the plane is sold out. That is not going to happen," I said.

We sat for forty minutes. Last call to board the plane was announced. "Kathryn Gregory to the podium, Kathryn Gregory to the podium, please."

"This is my upgrade," she sang as we ran up to the counter.

I rolled my eyes, but in my heart, I had a feeling she was right.

"Mrs. Gregory, it seems we have oversold this flight, and we would like to offer you a first-class upgrade free of charge if you give up your coach seat."

"Of course! That's great! Thank you!" Kathy was beaming, and I was incredulous.

I've seen God restore bodies and minds with miracle healings including my own, and yet I could not believe for a first-class upgrade. Yep, pretty clear here that I needed more healing.

Kathy grabbed her new upgraded ticket and looked from me to the gate agent. "What about my friend? We had seats in coach next to each other. Did she also get an upgrade?"

"Name, miss?" the agent asked me.

"Joanne Moody," I said as my mouth twitched. I was so convicted that I had watched Kathy with faith in action, and I had chosen not to participate.

"No, I'm sorry, Mrs. Moody. There is no upgrade for you."

I smiled at the agent, and I heard in my mind, *"By the measure of your faith...."*

The moment was iconic. I was smacked in the head with my own humanity and wishy-washy belief.

The irony continued. Kathy's seat originally ticketed next to mine in coach remained empty the entire 18-hour flight to San Francisco. I burst out laughing at the gigantic ways the Lord teaches me things. He blessed me even in my unbelief because I had two seats to stretch out on. The goodness and mercy of God. Truth be told, I guess my personality is a bit extreme and the Lord uses supreme measures to invite me to greater faith.

I thought and prayed a lot during that flight. *Lord, draw me into you in greater intimacy so that I will always have faith to believe for the impossible with consistency.*

Due to many other instances like the no first-class upgrade, I am learning more of the magnitude of God's love and trust in us. So, it was with a new level of faith that Kathy and I began walking into the Virgin Atlantic terminal in London Heathrow airport on that Tuesday morning. We lugged our bulging suitcases, but we carried wide open hearts to pray for anyone God would highlight. There was an excitement matched with expectancy brewing in both of our hearts. We checked our baggage and headed toward the escalator on the hunt for coffee.

As we neared the escalator, I noticed a dark-haired woman in her early thirties sitting against a large pillar in the main lobby. Her suitcases were all around her splayed out in disarray, and her carry-on bag was open in front of her crossed legs. Tingling radiated in my hands. I have come to know this is the Holy Spirit's presence for healing.

In my mind I asked the Lord, *What is going on with her?*

I saw a vision in front of me like a quick movie. The woman was a bit younger and on horseback. I watched the horse rear up on its hind legs, and the young woman fell to the ground and her body lay unnaturally twisted. I heard the Holy Spirit say, *Her back was broken, and she has had many surgeries. She is in the kind of pain you used to be in.* My heart filled to overflowing with compassion.

I looked at Kathy, and she nodded.

As we approached the woman, it was obvious she had been crying. Her back was against the pillar with her head tilted back, eyes closed.

"Excuse me," I blurted as I made my way toward her.

Her eyes opened, and she looked at me.

"I am sorry to bother you, but do you have really severe back pain?"

Her mouth dropped open and her eyes began to fill with tears. "How do you know that?" She touched the corner of her eyes with her fingertips.

"We are ministers, and we are practicing hearing the Lord, and we felt that He said you have severe back pain because you were thrown from a horse and you've had many surgeries. We believe the Lord will heal you right now. He healed me of nerve damage lasting almost fifteen years and thirteen surgeries. Now we run around the world praying for people and watching the Lord do that for others." The power of the testimony releases faith.

"Oh my gosh, I can't believe this. Yes, yes, please pray for me," she said as the avalanche of tears ran down her cheeks.

"What's your name?" Kathy said.

"Phoebe, I'm called Phoebe."

"Phoebe, if ten was the worst pain you can imagine being in and zero is no pain, what level is your pain now?" I asked.

"It's always twelve or more. I can't even take higher level of drugs." I knew what that was like. My heart welled again in the compassion of Jesus.

"I'm going to put my hand on your back, is that okay?" As I slid my hand between her back and the pillar, Kathy squatted down to join me. "Holy Spirit, thank You for being here to heal Phoebe. In the Name of Jesus Christ, we take authority over this pain." Before I continued, I felt a nudge from the Lord to ask Phoebe if she blamed herself for the accident.

Her audible wail and fresh tears told the story.

"Phoebe, would you be willing to forgive yourself?"

She nodded.

As I led her to break off the self-condemnation, we continued to the prayer for her spine. "Thank You, Lord that You have removed the right of the enemy to afflict Phoebe. We command by the blood of Jesus for this spine to be made whole now. All trauma, pain, and injury to the nerves, vertebrae, discs, tendons, ligaments, and cartilage be healed now in the Name of Jesus. Thank You, Holy Spirit. Thank You, Lord, for Your healing angels."

Phoebe gasped. "I can feel my back on fire! What is going on?"

Kathy laughed. "That's the love of God healing your spine. Can you stand up and see how you are? Move around?" Kathy and I helped Phoebe to her feet, and she shook under the presence of the Lord.

"I don't have any pain! What? This is crazy! God sent you! God sent you! You have no idea! Oh my gosh! What?"

Kathy and I squealed in delight at the Lord's mighty love. We were in total awe. Right there at London Heathrow, Jesus performed a miracle and used ordinary people like us. Incredible.

Phoebe continued bending and hopping, dancing, and crying. She reached into her open carry on and snatched her pink cell phone. "You can't leave. Please stay, I have to have you speak to my fiancé. He's a Christian!"

I looked at Kathy, and we both broke into chuckles again.

Phoebe hit a contact in her phone. "Babe, oh my gosh, babe! You are never going to believe what just happened. I am at the airport still, and I just got healed! My back, my back has no pain!" Kathy and I could hear shouts from the phone. "Will you talk to this lady? I want her to know how much you've prayed!"

The phone was placed in my hand. "Uh, hello? This is Jo."

"Jo, my name is Chris, and I live in Arizona and I believe in Jesus." He gulped through tears and run-on sentences. I thought he would jump through the phone. "Phoebe is my fiancée, and we are supposed to be married in a week. Oh my God! Oh my God! I can't believe it. I've been praying! She has been trying to board a plane for three weeks, but her pain is so high that each time she tries she is incapacitated with unbearable pain and has to go back home. I was losing heart that she would ever make it here, but I have been praying and praying that God would send her a miracle, so we can be together. I love her so much, but I know that God loves her more than me. Even when she didn't have faith, I just kept praying and wow! This is the miracle! Thank you, thank you!" He was gasping for breath through his tears.

My own eyes overflowed down my face. *Lord, you are beyond words.*

"Hey, Chris, it is us who need to thank you. Because of your prayers of intercession, the Lord prompted us to stop for Phoebe. We are the ones who are grateful and beyond awestruck at the faithfulness and kindness of God." I handed Phoebe back her phone, and we hugged her as she continued to speak to her fiancé about the next available flight.

"Never ever will I grow tired of this, Kath." My cheeks hurt from smiling despite the tears in my eyes at the goodness of God.

"Jo, let's see who else God is on before we board in two hours," she said.

"Absolutely!" I responded as we rode up the escalator. Together we turned to look over our shoulders at Phoebe, still waving her arms and hopping around—filled to overflowing with faith as she expressed her joy to her love on the phone.

May Phoebe come to know You intimately, Jesus, and share her testimony with everyone so You will be famous. She is only just beginning to understand the power of Your love and what faith can do. Draw her into You, Lord, and continue to give her revelation after revelation of Your greatness.

I hold fast to Proverbs 25:2: *"It is the glory of God to conceal a matter and the glory of kings to search it out"* (TLV).

Think about that for a moment. God isn't purposefully hiding revelation or healing from us. He calls us royalty. We are His kings. And it is our invitation to come into deeper fellowship with Him to find the revelatory truth—His truth that will set us free. When we begin to learn and embrace that we as believers are the heirs of Christ and therefore in unity with Him, there is so much more for us.

In Phoebe's case, she blamed herself for 10 years that if she had been more aware of the horse or a better rider, she would not have been injured. By believing that the accident was caused by her presumed negligence and lack of skill, Phoebe believed that God would pass her by and choose not to heal her—such a tragedy and such a common position for so many who are suffering trials of many kinds. God does not withhold blessing from us. But sometimes as we blame ourselves, we get in the way of His healing love through our self-judgment and criticism. God is not a respecter of persons (see Acts 10:34), meaning He loves all of His children equally, and His desire is to bring healing and wholeness to us.

What's Next Activation

— Prayer —

Be it physical, emotional, or spiritual pain, God is more than able to bring abounding grace, healing, and answers for whatever ails us. Perhaps, you are struggling financially, and you have not been the best steward of money in your lifetime. Though we will have consequences for wrong living, it is not the heart of God to punish or withhold blessing when we have repented and turned to Him. Maybe, you became injured because of a situation you blame yourself for like Phoebe. It is our hearts that God is concerned with, and I invite you now to pray.

> *Holy Spirit, where I have judged and blamed myself, would You show me? Here and now, Lord, I offer my life to You again. You said that You did not come to condemn me, so I refuse to condemn myself. I break the words I have thought and spoken over myself in the Name of Jesus. Lord, I take authority over any assignment of*

darkness to separate me from the healing love of Jesus because of what I used to think about myself. I invite You to take over every part of my heart, Holy Spirit. I give You full access. Heal my thinking and my body. Thank You for making all things new in me. My old self is dead. It is no longer I who live but Christ who lives in me. In Him, I am a brand-new creation, wholly accepted and dearly loved by my heavenly Father. Amen.

Give It Away

Who are those around you suffering physically, emotionally, or spiritually? As you have experienced the extraordinary story of Phoebe and prayed through your own trials, how can you give away what you have just received? Who needs your intercession and the healing touch of Jesus? Remember that in Matthew 10:8 Jesus commanded us to heal the sick—and not just pray for the sick but to know His resurrection power to bring complete transformation.

8

Flying with Jesus

MIRACLES ARE A RETELLING IN SMALL LETTERS
OF THE VERY SAME STORY WHICH IS WRITTEN
ACROSS THE WHOLE WORLD IN LETTERS TOO
LARGE FOR SOME OF US TO SEE.

C. S. LEWIS, *GOD IN THE DOCK*

Because our Agape team travels the majority of the year, I often encourage the ministry team to look around the airports and ask the Lord if there is anyone He would like to touch there. I tell them, "You will likely never see these people again, so it is a great time to practice hearing the Lord and releasing His healing love!"

What once was intimidating to so many on our team has become a regular part of our mission trips. We have hundreds of airport stories involving salvations, healing, and miracles and each of them is reflective of the Lord reaching down through ordinary people to tangibly love a precious son or daughter. It is true we rarely see those folks again but the memory of how God touched and transformed them is never forgotten. *"'Unless you people see signs and wonders,' Jesus told him, 'you will never believe'"* (John 4:48 NIV).

My dear friend and fellow Agape team member, Kathi Frye, and I were headed to Belfast, Ireland, and landed in the early morning mist at London Heathrow airport. We had more than three hours before our connecting flight. Before I tell you what happened, I think it's important that you know about Kathi. Her most important value in life is to be known by our heavenly Father, followed by a ferocity for her family to understand Jesus' love and forgiveness through her expression of His wisdom in their everyday lives. Finally, Kathi gives away all she has been poured into by our Father in Heaven to every person the Holy Spirit directs her to pray for. I never grow tired of watching how the Lord releases His love through each member of our team as each is unique and beautiful. Sharing a common bond of laughter, we have a joy for the Lord that continues to take us on countless adventures surprising us all along the way. We hold fast to Colossians 3:17: *"And whatever you do or say, do it as a representative of the Lord Jesus, giving thanks through him to God the Father."*

"Want to get a coffee?" I asked Kathi while we headed to the customs booths.

"Well, yes. Maybe two of them. We have a ton of time." She laughed.

"Okay, that Nero's coffee place we like is upstairs and out the main doors. Let's go there." I caught up with her again after luggage recheck, and we walked into Nero's coffee shop and stood in a short line. I looked up as I heard a conversation between two Heathrow police officers in front of us.

A red-haired, freckled faced officer pushed up his hat. "You know, it just hurts all the time. It's these bloody packs we have to wear, and it's not getting better. I even bought new shoes."

The brown-haired, brown-eyed taller of the two remarked, "Me too, sick of it, but I'm sicker of listening to you whine about your back every day."

With a shout, the barista broke into their conversation over the whirring and spitting of the espresso machine. "What can I get you guys?"

The officers turned away from each other to face the barista in the brown Nero's shirt, and I felt the Holy Spirit at the same time Kathi did. We smiled at each other with the knowing that only comes from having experienced the faithfulness of God in everyday life through situations just like this.

I tapped the red-haired officer on the shoulder. "So, you have back pain, huh?"

He looked startled.

"I heard you guys talking about your back pain."

The officers looked a little embarrassed.

"I'm Jo, and this is Kathi."

"Hello," the red-haired officer replied in an Irish accent. The other nodded.

"So, we are ministers, and we believe Jesus heals today, as we have both experienced miracles and seen thousands healed. Can we pray for your backs?"

They looked at each other with eyebrows raised. The Irish officer responded, "Right here?"

"We can just order our coffees and move down to the end of the counter there." Before they had time to stop us, we ordered and paid and moved to the end of the counter, where I stuck my hand up behind the flak jacket of the Irish officer. "I promise this will only take a sec, and nobody will even know we are praying. I promise we won't be weird."

"This is already weird!" he said.

I knew the Lord was about to do something amazing, so I ignored him.

"Father, in the Name of Jesus I command all back pain to leave this body and for the effects of carrying this heavy armor each day to end the pattern of pain. I command the core muscles to strengthen and the entire body to be healed in Jesus' Name." I watched his face from the side as he faced his partner.

"What!? I feel a wee bit of heat! What's happening?!" He gasped.

"See how it feels." I smiled.

His partner's face was incredulous. Eyes wide as saucers.

"It's almost gone!" the Irish officer said.

The barista looked over at us and walked our coffees to the counter in front of us. He looked over his shoulder once more as he walked back to the cashier station, perplexed at why my hand was up the back of a police officer's flak jacket. I laughed with Kathi.

"Okay, praise God," I said. "I'm going to pray for you once more, and then you will have no more pain because God sure loves you." I could feel the heat coming through his shirt and see the sweat formed over his lip. "Any spirit of infirmity and all pain. leave now in the Name of Jesus Christ."

At that, the Irish officer began moving and bending. "I can't believe it! I'm going home to tell me wife I've been touched!"

We laughed.

"Just say, 'Thanks, Jesus, for my healing.'"

"Thanks, Jesus, for my healing. This is just amazing!"

"Now your turn." Kathi said to the brown-haired officer. "Is it okay if I put my hand on your back under your jacket?" Kathi is so much more polite than I am.

"It's yeah...sure, it's fine. This is crazy."

As Kathi prayed, the red-haired officer kept twisting and bending, remarking all the while that God is incredible to do this.

The brown-haired officer, who was healed after a few moments, said, "I can't believe it. God is in this. I'm going back to church. I don't have pain, and still the best part is I don't have to hear you carry on about your back anymore!" His red-haired partner made a face at him.

Both of them bent and moved, smiling and exclaiming what a day they were having. "We don't know how to thank you," they said almost in unison.

"No thanks necessary. Thank God. He's the One who did it all. We just had fun watching Him do it. Have a great day!" We walked off to a table, and they did the same in the back of the coffee shop.

Close to thirty minutes later, they approached our table nearer the front of the shop. "So, do you girls come here often?" one of them said.

I burst out laughing. "You mean like hanging around the airport praying for people?" Everyone laughed. I had an instantaneous impression from the Holy Spirit that they were trying to figure out how we could pray for their other officer friends who also suffered severe back pain wearing a twenty-seven-pound pack and walking on concrete floors all day for years and years.

Kathi set her coffee down and said, "We travel through here many times a year but at all different times. We are headed to Ireland."

"Me homeland!" exclaimed the redheaded officer. "When will you come back through?"

"A week from tomorrow," I said.

"We will look for you, and if you have other officers who need healing, you can let us know."

"How great would that be, Tom?" he said to his partner.

"You know, you guys can pray for them yourselves," I said. "You heard how simple Jesus makes it for us."

They both looked at each other and shrugged their shoulders. "We'd rather run into you girls again. This day changed our lives. Thank you again."

"Hope we see you again. God bless you."

"And you," they responded as they turned to leave.

"Never gets old, huh, Jo?" Kathi said.

I laughed. "Never gets old. How great You are, God. Thank You, Holy Spirit."

We picked up our carry-on luggage and headed to our gate.

A week later we flew back through London Heathrow and into another terminal. We looked around for the officers or any others but didn't find them. The mystery of God is to simply partner with His invitation to do what Jesus said to do. Much of the time we won't see the people again, but we continually rejoice at the great and marvelous things the Lord has done.

At 5:00 a.m. on a crisp early autumn morning in Pennsylvania, one member of our Agape team and I returned our rental car and stepped into the terminal for our 7:00 a.m. flight back to California. We had just come from a full week at Global Awakening's Voice of the Apostles near Harrisburg. The airport was almost empty, so we found our way to TSA security in a matter of minutes. Entering the area between the miles of black webbing anchored by chrome stanchions, I paid little attention to the area around me as I prepared to pull out liquids and my laptop.

"Oh my gosh, it's you!" said a gray-haired man wearing a lime-green jacket who had come up behind my friend Kathy and me in the security line.

You'll remember Kathy from the first-class upgrade testimony in the previous chapter. I knew we were in for another surprise from the Lord.

"What?" I laughed. The man fell down half laughing, and I could now feel the presence of the Holy Spirit moving powerfully over us.

Kathy cracked up. "Oh my gosh! What's happening right now?"

I was still laughing when the lime-green jacket man spoke again.

"You're that woman from the conference! Every time I got near you, the Holy Spirit knocked me out. So don't touch me!" He guffawed and howled.

Kathy and I were up next in the security line, and with no other people in line behind the man, I realized how conspicuous we must have looked. "Hey! I'm not touching you at all, you're already wasted!"

Shrieks of laughter burst from all three of us.

"Kathy, we have got to get it together here. I don't want to be arrested by the security people."

We turned away from the lime-green jacket man and straightened up.

I looked ahead and saw a TSA agent approaching me.

As soon as he looked me in the eyes he yelled, "Whoa! Will you back up, please?" He held his hand up, motioning me to stop. The remark and his action were bizarre since I was not stepping forward and there was not a soul in front of me.

I knew it was a convergence of the Holy Spirit coming onto this agent because I watched his eyes when he locked eyes with me. I've seen the Lord do this before.

In a flash I heard the Holy Spirit say, *Tell him he really likes dogs and dogs have changed his life.*

Lord, are you kidding me right now? I am just trying not to get arrested and now You want me to say that to this guy who appears to be the head honcho since his gold badge is huge and says Supervisor? Please, let me get through the security check. I didn't hear a response from the Lord until I grabbed my bag from the conveyor belt.

Tell him what I told you.

I looked over at Kathy, who was now placing her stuff on the conveyer belt, followed by lime-green jacket man. Both of them were still howling in laughter.

I know what it means to partner with the invitation of the Holy Spirit but truthfully, I wonder sometimes about His timing. I felt the weightiness of His presence again. *Okay, Lord but we need the green jacket guy to get through here, so he doesn't fall over and make a scene.* I looked over at Kathy as lime-green jacket man reclaimed his belongings. We shared a knowing look and an understanding of what the

Lord desired to do because we know the Holy Spirit loves to encourage people.

When our jovial new friend walked toward us, we laid our hands on his shoulders and asked the Lord to increase His presence. Lime-green jacket man fell over onto the nearest wooden bench under the presence of God and we left him there.

"This is ridiculous!" I said to Kathy while we burst into sniggering fits of laughter.

We made our way over to the central TSA desk where the supervisor was standing.

Okay, Lord. I'll do what you asked.

The supervisor turned to face me as I approached.

I cleared my throat. "Um...this might be totally weird, but I believe you really like dogs, and dogs have changed your life."

The supervisor shifted in his stance, and his eyes flashed a moment of vulnerability. "I do really like dogs, and dogs have changed my life. Who are you?"

"I'm nobody, but I felt like God asked me to say that to you and this: You're not from here, you moved here to help your family member, and you're having a hard time. You're wondering if things will get better for you. God hasn't forgotten about you, and He is very proud of you for making the sacrifice of this move." Words flowed like a gushing river as tears leaked out of the bewildered brown eyes staring at me with disbelief. His cheeks were wet with little streams that ended in the supervisor's sandy blond-gray beard.

"This is crazy," he said. "You don't even know. Oh my gosh, what's happening? I'm not from here. I moved here to take care of my mom. I was a canine police officer in California, and when I moved here, I had to give that up. And this job was the only thing available. I miss my dog, I can't have a dog here, and dogs are my life. I have been so unhappy. I just can't believe God told you all that."

"Well, you might find this even weirder. We're from California."

The look on his face was incredulous.

"I'm from Citrus Heights. That's where I was a canine officer for twenty-seven years," he pointed out.

"How wild!" I laughed. "Kathy and I are from Roseville and Rocklin, just down the freeway from Citrus Heights."

The supervisor looked like he might fall over from the impact of the presence of the Holy Spirit.

I looked into his eyes once more. "I pray right now that you are lifted up and encouraged that the Lord will honor your sacrifice to do what was right in His eyes. I believe you not only will have another dog, but the Lord is moving powerfully on your behalf, or He would not have sent us here. Lord, bless this son of yours and give Him the desires of His heart in the Name of Jesus."

Fresh tears and a nod in agreement was the only response from this precious man. The Lord was doing something divine in the middle of the airport security.

"I don't know what to say. Do you have a business card?" he asked.

I smiled and handed him one. "This is all thanks to the Lord, not me. It was an honor to hear His heart for you. Have an amazing day." With that Kathy and I walked away.

Just then the lime-green jacket man walked toward us. "You guys looked busy over there," he said. "Wow, God is really moving in this airport!"

We broke into shouts of joy and turned to head to our gate when we heard hysterics and shrieking coming from the TSA security line. "Oh my gosh, it's our team! I would recognize that crazy joy anywhere."

I turned and saw several members of our Agape Freedom Fighters ministry team, along with Leif Hetland and his assistant, Scotty, moving through the security screening. Leif had been one of the speakers at Voice of the Apostles.

As Scotty and Leif walked toward me, the supervisor approached them. "Sir, you have something in your bag we need to inspect."

I smiled at the supervisor, who quickly wiped his eyes and looked away, trying to focus on his job.

"I think I left scissors in your bag, Leif. Sorry about that," Scotty said.

I burst out laughing. "Well, Leif, I think this is a God setup between you and the supervisor there who is about to unpack your bag."

Leif smiled, and his eyebrows shot up to his hairline in amusement. "Oh! He is a 'chair number one man,' eh?" Leif and Scotty guffawed, and we all felt the power of God's presence increase again.

Leif Hetland has an amazing "chair number one" analogy about people who—despite what is happening to them and around them—remain steadfast, focused on the Lord and what He says. They seat themselves in a place of honor, respect, joy, and love, and they choose to place their trust in our heavenly Father, reflecting His same attributes to everyone we come in contact with.

When Leif walked over to the supervisor and began to prophesy, the supervisor looked up at me and asked, "Who are you people?" We giggled and walked away as Leif—even while his bag was being searched for the infamous scissors—began to pray for him.

Our team eventually made it through security and into the gate area with stories of praying and prophesying over the agents at the Delta ticket counter in the main lobby of the airport. They invited one of the agents to a conference we were having a few weeks from then. Exhilaration and mirth poured out from all of us as we celebrated the goodness of God, and soon everyone waiting for the same flight was watching.

The world needs Jesus, and the joy of the Lord is our strength (see Neh. 8:10) as we move in unity with Him.

Luke 4:18-19 in *The Passion Translation* says, *"The Spirit of the Lord is upon me, and He has anointed me to be hope for the poor, freedom for the brokenhearted, and new eyes for the blind, and to preach to prisoners, 'You are set free!' I have some to share the message of Jubilee, for the time of God's great acceptance has begun."* In this passage, Jesus announced what had just been ushered into existence through the new covenant.

As His beloved followers it is our privilege and honor to accept the invitation of the Holy Spirit to set captives free wherever we go. It might not seem convenient or even wise from a natural perspective, but God desires that all people be saved (see 1 Tim. 2:4), and He wishes to use us as His ambassadors of hope and reconciliation in Jesus. Love is expressed in the most unique ways through the God who sees and knows the struggles of every life.

What's Next Activation

— *Prayer* —

Lord, I confess I feel inadequate and even disqualified to step forward and release prophetic words over people or to pray for their healing. But today, I am choosing to believe You at Your word. You said that signs, won- ders, and miracles follow all who believe and that in Your Name I would prophesy, heal the sick, and cause demons to flee. I believe You! I reject every thought or word I have had that tries to disqualify me or cause me to shrink back from what You have invited me into as Your child. Today, I ask for a specific word and invitation from You to pray for someone in front of me. Lord, teach me Your ways, let me walk in Your truth, and give me an undivided heart that I would fear Your Name and not fear other people or making mistakes in learning to hear You. I ask You to take over my heart and use me today to encourage someone. Help me to understand that prophecy is encouragement and a simple kindness changes a life. Holy Spirit, I give You permission to invade my life both when I am awake and when I am asleep. Thank You for opening my eyes to see and my ears to hear all that You have in store for those around me. For the glory of Jesus Christ. Amen.

Give It Away

Sit quietly with the Holy Spirit and ask Him to bring to mind a time when He told you something about someone. Perhaps, you never realized it was the Lord at that time. Some of these moments might include an overwhelming feeling you should text or call someone with an encouragement or other specific inclination. Ask Him now who He wants to use you to encourage today. Often just releasing the simple first impression or thought gives way to the next piece of information the Lord wants to give the person He has highlighted to you.

I would not have known the supervisor for TSA had moved across the country to help someone or that he could not have a dog now if I had not released first the original word of liking dogs and dogs changing his life. Faith comes by hearing, and as we release the first thing, faith is rising to receive the next thing. Faith rises in you and the one receiving the encouragement. Keep it simple. The keys are childlike faith and joy.

For those who already walk in step with the prophetic invitation of the Lord, ask the Holy Spirit to give you a new way to experience the prophetic for another person. Remember you have five senses and the spiritual realm of Jesus Christ is not limited to just feeling or hearing. Seeing, smell, taste, and touch are also available.

9

Horizontal People

I AM NOT LAZY, I JUST LIKE A LOT OF
HORIZONTAL LIFE PAUSES.

YOUR ECARDS

First Peter 2:1-4 says to abstain from the passions of the flesh that wage war against our souls. Scripture implores us to cease all malice, deceit, hypocrisy, envy, and slander so we can grow up in our salvation. We are directed to embrace that we are being built up as living stones as a spiritual house to collectively be the royal priesthood of God, offering our lives as perfect and acceptable in Christ. Our calling as believers in Christ is to mature. Ephesians 4:13-15 gives us a great framework for understanding spiritual maturity and its importance. *The Passion Translation* says,

---

These grace ministries will function until we all attain oneness into the faith, until we all experience the fullness of what it means to know the Son of God, and finally we become one into a perfect man with the full dimensions of spiritual maturity and fully developed into the abundance of Christ. And then our immaturity will end! And we will not be easily shaken by trouble, nor led astray by novel teachings or by the false doctrines of deceivers who teach clever lies. But instead we will remain strong and always sincere in our love as we express the truth. All our direction and ministries will flow from Christ and lead us deeper into him, the anointed Head of his body, the church.

Without maturation we cannot truly know Jesus, and we will be easily disturbed by trials and upheaval, lacking in discernment. The strength to walk out our calling and to obtain all the Lord has planned for each of us is found in the process of maturation. At the risk of repeating myself, I want to underline the importance of intimate connection with God. This is where maturation starts and grows. Of course, we must practice spiritual disciplines as part of the divine connection of intimacy with God. The study of Scripture—not in place of intimacy with Christ but as part of the divine connection. Worship, prayer, intercession with gratitude, and soaking in the presence of God are all ways in which we grow up in Jesus. The Holy Spirit illuminates the Word of God, causing our hearts to be continually awestruck at the majesty of the Almighty.

We are like a well-watered garden because Jesus is the living water. Think about spiritual disciplines as the Miracle-Gro for our souls. Miracle-Gro for your garden plants causes prolific growth and health. I am not sure what chemicals are in those bright blue granules, but they work. With Miracle-Gro, my gardenia bush produces so many blossoms that my entire backyard is filled with their sweet fragrance. The presence of the Holy Spirit, the Word of God, and the practice of worship, prayer, fasting, and soaking with God's presence are the right recipe for our prolific growth. Transformation happens through process. May we be overcome by Him and release the sweet aroma of Heaven to all of those around us.

One more point about maturation. The blessings, unique gifts, and empowerment on your life is called anointing. Anointing grows when the inner man is transformed. Anointing is the unity and demonstration of the Word of God and the Spirit of God in the life of the believer. Any outward manifestation of supernatural anointing in our lives comes from the inner transformation through both the Word of God and the Holy Spirit. Anointing matures as you mature. Don't make the mistake of desiring greater anointing without passionately pursing growing up in the Lord. Anointing without maturity is not sustainable. A weak foundation in us will not support the level of anointing the Lord has planned to pour out through us so that the world knows He is God.

Maturing is our supernatural reality as children of God, and it's our inheritance in Christ. It also happens to be our purpose upon the earth as salt and light. But, let's face it. Sometimes, we are not ourselves. Have you ever had one of those days when your flesh seems to hijack your mouth? Wow. I know the pattern. When I'm exhausted, the filter over my mouth develops holes, and I can be incredibly immature. On those less than delightful days, doubt, fear, or even apathy can creep in like deadly spiders. Their sticky webs can develop in the corners of my mind, if I let the darkness remain. I know I have developed a web if I start to compare. I can find all kinds of things to compare and none of them are good. Comparison for me is a cancerous thought process that disrupts unity through dishonor and quenches the Holy Spirit.

You are probably more mature than I am. I have learned that comparison stunts my growth and is an invitation to rebellion. I believe it can be such a stronghold that it thwarts destiny and defiles many around the one comparing. Yikes. It is like a viper. When I compare, I have pulled up a seat at the enemy's table. And the fruit from dining there is strife, contempt, and envy.

In the years of managing people and being placed in roles of leadership over large groups of people, both secular and Christian, I have not observed a great deal of difference between Christians and non-Christians in the area of comparison. That is not a fun sentence to type. It has grieved me over the years because I have been that person who has compared, and I have warranted my actions because I felt an injustice had been done to me or someone else. The unfortunate thing about being a justice-oriented person is that when we don't seek the Lord who is the God of justice, we wear the weight and outcome of our judgment. But, when we decide to lay down our own criticism and inquire of the Lord in the matter at hand, we find mercy there and it stops our compulsion to want to step in front of Jesus and act as judge for ourselves.

I love the Kingdom family of God. Having the privilege of building people up into functional teams through their identity in Christ and watching them soar together with the power of the Lord's love through the Holy Spirit is what I know I was born to do. Under a sense of spiritual urgency, I have asked the Lord for help in bringing influence into the Church to accelerate the raising up of more mature Kingdom family teams delivered of the spirit of comparison.

I remember praying once, *Lord, help me. I need wisdom from You for breakthrough in the area of understanding comparison and discord.*

I heard the Holy Spirit say, *Study the meaning of horizontal and you will know.*

The Lord makes me smile. He is so incredibly creative and solution oriented, and I marvel at the way He offers exactly what we need if we just take the time to ask.

Before I launched into the study of what horizontal meant, I felt led from the Holy Spirit to review and keep open in front of me First Corinthians 12:12-15, 17-20 (TPT):

Just as the human body is one, though it has many parts that together form one body, so too is Christ. For by one Spirit we were immersed and mingled into one single body. And no matter what our status—whether we are Jews or non-Jews, oppressed or free—we are all privileged to drink deeply of the same Holy Spirit.
In fact, the human body is not one single part, but rather many parts mingled into one. So, if the foot were to say,

"Since I'm not a hand, I'm not part of the body," it's forgetting that it is still a vital part of the body. ...

*Think of it this way, if the whole body were just an eyeball, how would it hear sounds? And if the whole body were just an ear, how would it smell different fragrances? But God has carefully designed each member and placed it in the body to function as he desires. A **diversity** is required, for if the body consisted of one single part, there wouldn't be a body at all! So now we see there are many differing parts and functions, but one body.*

The meaning of the word *horizontal* is:

1. Parallel to the horizon, at right angles to the vertical
2. Involving social groups of equal status
3. Junction of earth and sky
4. Being in a prone or supine position; recumbent

Synonyms: Parallel, level, even, straight, flush

Okay, Lord, this is a lot of information. Help me out. What is most important about this?

I had an imprint in my mind in a split second: *Horizontal people groups are all the same status. Created and treated equally. Assumed important as individuals for the greater whole. Now, look up the meaning of vertical people groups.*

Father, I know that is something I have heard about American politics, but I don't know what it means.

Though I did not have another answer, I felt the encouragement of the Lord.

Maybe you already know what I learned. Vertical people groups are members of a different social status. There is a whole lot of that happening in America these days. The vertical people group has a clear agenda. Many political groups often categorize themselves as vertical groups because it has come to mean a group of people willing to work with those different from them. Having people willing to work with others who are diversified sounds appealing until you understand their hidden agenda. The vertical group position is not one of truth. Manipulation is their foundation for they assert themselves as superior over others and desire to control freedom. Underneath what is being said by the vertical people group is an ideology that believes they are right, and everyone else is wrong. No matter what you believe, if you do not follow what they believe, you are vilified. The vertical group member will stand next to you as long as it takes to convince you to believe in what they are selling and align with you until you come under their influence and control. Through subtle maneuvering and often using fear as a catalyst, the vertical person will eventually cause all those who are unaware within their influence to leave their beliefs. You'll find vertical people shaped by the political and religious spirits. When these spirits of disunity are present there is suspicion, control, and fear, subtlety leading people to create an "us and them" mentality. Total control is their objective. It is the blueprint of the Kingdom of darkness.

When learning about vertical people, I sat quietly reflecting what the Lord was saying—*Kingdom people are horizontal people*—the Holy Spirit gave me a picture of God's children laid back and resting on Jesus. Trust and childlike faith.

Lord, show me more. I want to understand.

I felt the love and presence of God in my office as He spoke.

Kingdom people are a horizontal people who stand between the earth and heavens with the Holy Spirit connecting the heavenly realms to earth through them. They bring the supernatural reality of the Kingdom into fruition here and now. To bring the glorious message of Jesus to every tribe, tongue, and nation.

A vision unfolded before me like a dream, but I was not asleep. I saw the Bride of Christ standing shoulder to shoulder across the whole earth and arrows being shot through them through words, action, and divisiveness. The flaming arrows came down in a vertical line and interrupted the line of unified believers. These arrows were actually people or groups of people proclaiming to be one and agreeing with the mission and vision Christ set for us, but at the core they wanted control and recognition. And their motives were centered on what they believed they deserved because of their position, status, or gifting. They asserted themselves into the mix without regard to the good of the whole, the value of each individual, or the larger story of God He had woven together through the unity of His children and call to renew the Bride of Christ.

Next, I heard this:

When we view the family of God as a vertical people, we are agreeing with the lie that some are more important than others or that we are more important than a brother or sister. This is a direct contradiction to Scripture in First Corinthians 12.

In First Corinthians 12:4-7 (ESV) Paul says, *"Now, there are varieties of gifts, but the same Spirit; and there are varieties of service, but the same Lord; and there are varieties of activities, but it is the same God who empowers them all in everyone. To each is given the manifestation of the Spirit for the common good. Everyone is in this together expressing God in unique ways through the power of the Holy Spirit all for the common good of all people."*

Paul is identifying true unity in the people of God and expressing that unity is built on the premise that we are all equally valuable. A person of God is a horizontal person. I come and stand next to you with the understanding that we are all equal and all priceless. As I am positioned with you, I am trying to share your worldview, bring out the best in you, and work together with you for the building up of the whole Body of Christ. My desire is authentic collaboration, to join you in what you're doing and promote Jesus as central to all we are doing together.

I sat marveling at what I had heard from the Holy Spirit and the contrast Paul paints of true Kingdom unity in First Corinthians 12. I realized that popular culture categorizes all manner of vertical people groups based on popularity, status, position, wealth, name, origin, gender, nationality, denomination, and many more things. Sadly, we allow that same divisive spiritual climate into the Body of Christ—completely missing that we are called to be a horizontal people.

For centuries, in Western Christianity we have placed the burden of problem-solving and load bearing upon one pastor or one couple within the church body because we view some as more important and qualified. Every person, believing in Jesus Christ—no matter their education, station, socioeconomic group or earning potential—is qualified because Jesus is the qualifier. God's Word declares the truth of who we are and what we are called for: *"You are a chosen race, a royal priesthood, a holy nation, a people for his own possession, that you may proclaim the excellencies of him who called you out of darkness into his marvelous light"* (1 Peter 2:9 ESV). Every single believer is a royal priest possessed by God to proclaim the Lord's excellence. In John 15:16, Jesus declares that He chose and appointed us to bear fruit. If our mindset of inequality produces inertia in our lives, we are hardly declaring the excellence of the Lord or producing fruit. I'm convinced this is why the enemy works overtime in the area of comparison within the Body of Christ.

The idea that only a few are qualified perpetuates our lack of understanding that according to Scripture, all believers are chosen, called, appointed, and given gifts to mature the Bride of Christ and ready her for her King. Every person should be treated as exceptional because to treat them as ordinary means we have already dishonored them. When we devalue another because we view them as less than, we have refused to place them in their position of influence that God created in advance for them to fulfill in His Kingdom story. Read First Corinthians 12:13-19 from *The Message*.

Each of us is now part of his resurrection body, refreshed and sustained at one fountain—his Spirit—where we all come to drink. The old labels we once used to define our-selves—labels like Jew or Greek, slave or free—are no longer useful. We need something larger, more comprehensive.

I want you to think about how all of this makes you more significant, not less. A body isn't just a single part blown up into something huge. It's all the different-but-similar parts all arranged and functioning together....As it is, we see that God has carefully placed each body part right where he wanted it....But I also want you to think about how this keeps your significance from getting blown up into self-importance. For no matter how significant you are, it is only because of what you are part of....No part is important on its own.

The rest of this section of First Corinthians 12 goes on to describe how we are to treat the weaker or some translations say "lower" parts. I was amused that *The Message* described what a body would be if it was just a giant eyeball or how it would function with no stomach but having great hair. I think you get the point.

God has given us the body to understand how we are to function together as the Church—His Bride. If one part is hurt, all hurt. If one part flourishes, all flourish: apostles, teachers, prophets, preachers, helpers, miracle workers, those who speak in tongues and those who interpret tongues, organizers. Not one is more important than the next. Paul follows all of this examination and exhortation with the entire 13th chapter of First Corinthians of what everything is about, love. For if we can do all of these things and have not love, we are nothing. Paul writes that love heals everything and champions all. That love gives generously and doesn't seek promotion.

My takeaway from being a horizontal people in Jesus is that as we spend time in the presence of the Lord—regularly pressing in for a deeper connection to His love—we begin to heal, change, and become transformed into His image as He said we would. This is the maturation process I was speaking about earlier, where anointing flourishes and unity becomes the foundation for revival. With our hearts molded like His, we can believe God and what He says about us and the one in front of us. This revelation of Kingdom truth impacts our viewpoint and value of a human life and only then is comparison put to death.

On a trip to an American city, our Agape Freedom Fighters team had ministered for a few days, and a little after 11 p.m. one night we decided to duck into a restaurant to grab dinner. The parking lot was busy, and as we exited the car, we were steeped in conversation.

Ed remarked. "That was something when that man's back and knees were healed after he forgave his father, huh?"

"Crazy," I said, "when he started doing deep knee squats on the platform. Come on, Jesus!"

As a team, we love celebrating all the Lord does through simple prayer and His extraordinary love.

We were moving toward the front door of the restaurant when I spotted a young man in his early twenties sitting on the ground. He was gaunt, dressed in combat fatigues, and had skin covered in black grime. He had seen hard times in the streets, and in his limp hands he held a sign that said, "Please help $."

"Here, son. God bless you." One of our team pressed money into his dirt-encrusted hand.

Most of the team followed Kyle into the restaurant. Kathi and I were a distance behind them when everything changed.

She squatted down in front of the young man and spoke softly. "Hi, I'm Kathi, and I am a mom. What's your name? Would you look at me?"

Head hung over his chest, the young man would not look up.

I squatted down beside him, recognizing the invitation of the Holy Spirit that Kathi had decided to partner with.

With the tender touch of a mother and the pure love of Christ, Kathi reached her hand under his chin and said, "Would you look at me, please?" He looked at her briefly and hung his head again.

She began to speak softly but with a heart exploding in Christ's love. "You're important. You are seen. You are priceless." She lifted his head again until her eyes—Jesus' eyes—locked with his.

I saw a spark of life in his eyes.

Tears began to flood his eyes. "I'm Zach."

With the fiery love of Jesus, Kathi continued, "Zach, you are not forgotten or abandoned. Our heavenly Father loves you so very much. You are so important to Him."

Tears rolled down my face as she held the young man's gaze.

The whole atmosphere was changed as the perfect love of the Father poured over Zach like fragrant perfume. Kathi simply did as the Holy Spirit instructed. No condemnation, no forceful evangelism but sowing seeds of Jesus' love. Zach was not our evangelism project. He wasn't clean, sober, or professing Jesus at that exact moment, but the Lord was clear on how to approach him. Treat him like he is part of the Kingdom—as priceless royalty. As one of God's horizontal people. He is not in a vertical group simply because of his addiction and sin. He is priceless now, not when he is sober. This precious boy needed to be seen and told the truth. We trust and pray for his complete healing and deliverance for he will never be the same.

How can anyone be left unmarked when the God of all the universe pours out love through the words, touch, and affection of a mom willing to stop for the one in front of her? In Titus 3:2-8 in *The Message*, Paul writes the truth for life.

God's people should be big hearted and courteous.

It wasn't so long ago that we ourselves were stupid and stubborn, easy marks for sin, ordered every which way by our glands, going around with a chip on our shoulder, hated and hating back. But when God, our kind and loving Savior God, stepped in, he saved us from all that. It was all his doing; we had nothing to do with it. He gave us a good bath, and we came out of it new people, washed inside and out by the Holy Spirit. Our Savior Jesus poured out new life so generously. God's gift has restored our relationship with him and given us back our lives. And there's more life to come—an eternity of life! You can count on this.

———— ••••• ————

Paul is calling us to grow up. To give away what we have been given. As mature believers we are called to put an end to quarrelsome talk and foolish arguments, an end to comparison and judgment. Encourage others to do the same. Respect and love people no matter where they are, help them and remember what Christ has done for us all. There is more than enough for all to take a place at the banqueting table of the Lord.

Heavenly Father, let that be our framework for how we live. No more comparison. No more vertical groups.

What's Next Activation

— Prayer —

Lord, You said that a Kingdom divided against itself cannot stand. Being a horizontal Kingdom person means I can look at everyone, no matter who they are, as priceless and equally valuable in Your eyes. I believe that each person is holy and set apart for Your glory. Lord Jesus, help me see my own obstacles to self-worth. Root out my prejudices and pitfalls. You said that no weapon of the enemy can prosper against me. I ask that

You be the Lord over any of the things I perceive limit me and cause me doubt. I give You my fear and insecurities. Jesus, remove from me a heart of criticism. Take my heart of stone and give me a heart of flesh. Fill my heart to overflowing with compassion and love so I will walk as You walk. Help me see those in bondage and fear as holy and righteous. Thank You that they are priceless to You and so am I. Lord, thank You that You will never condemn me. Therefore, I will choose not to condemn others. I choose to break any and all agreements with comparison. Draw me closer to You and help me believe Your love for others and for me is without measure or boundaries. Anoint me now with Your love, Father, and pour Your shalom peace over my mind, heart, and soul.

Give It Away

Next time you're out in public, ask the Holy Spirit to show you someone who needs to be seen and acknowledged. Be the love of Jesus and watch the Lord move through your unique expression of Him.

10

A Word in Season

LISTEN FOR GOD'S VOICE IN EVERYTHING
YOU DO, EVERYWHERE YOU GO; HE'S THE ONE
WHO WILL KEEP YOU ON TRACK.

PROVERBS 3:5 (MSG)

In the middle of a conference in Mustang, Oklahoma, the Holy Spirit broke out, and I was overwhelmed. I had prepared to speak on a topic I really felt the Lord had given to me when I heard the Holy Spirit say, *Lift up your arms and say My names in Hebrew.*

I had prayed a few times with some of the names of God in worship services and in my private adoration of the Lord, but this directive was new. *Yes, Lord*, I responded in my mind. The presence of God came like a blanket over the room as I lifted my arms and began praying the Hebrew names of God.

"Lord God, you are Yahweh, creator God. El Elyon, God of the universe, Elohim, Jehovah Shammah, Jehovah Nissi. The banner of love, Lord almighty, You are faithful, El Emunah. You alone are our refuge, Jehovah Machsi. You are El Shaddai, and we hide in the shadow of Your wings. You are the God who sees us, El Roi. You are Jeshua, Messiah, Savior, beloved Redeemer. You are El Bethel. Thank You, Holy Spirit, Ruach Hachodesh."

With every name of God, the presence of the Holy Spirit became greater. I walked down the center aisle with the people in attendance on either side. Some were already crumbling and shaking under the weight of His presence. Before I had a chance to think, out of my mouth flew, "The Lord is healing people right now!"

I stopped and turned to look at a woman in the center of a row on the left side. I couldn't reach her because the crowd was so thick. I stepped up on the chairs as everyone was standing and climbed over to her. "You have diabetes, and the Lord is healing you. Thank You, Jesus."

As I touched her shoulder, the Holy Spirit increased and she fell over into her chair.

Next the Holy Spirit highlighted a man in a green polo shirt and wire-frame glasses on the right side of the aisle. "You have had years of back pain and trauma," I said. "But in Jesus' Name the trauma is leaving you and your back pain is healed!"

He fell over.

The Lord continued telling me of specific medical conditions on different people, and with each word the person fell under the anointing of God. My legs were shaking beneath me because the presence of the Holy Spirit increased with every healing. There were angels around ministering in His glory and fire. I was undone.

I learned from my friend Blaine Cook to join God in what He is already doing. This means, do what He is leading you to do no matter what. When I used to try to do ministry in a specific order or give a certain message because that is what I believed the people needed to hear, I was not entirely cooperating with the Lord. The Lord is gracious and compassionate and very patient in teaching me, but there came a time when I finally gave up on self-reliance and made the decision to trust God. The Word says that God withholds no good thing from those who do what is right (see Ps. 84:11). His plans are perfect and although He blesses His children, at some point there is a choice to mature. I believe that obedience in Christ is partnership with the divine.

Why did it take me so long to do it?

Fear. There, I said it.

All of my life I have not wanted to be a disappointment to anyone in a position over me or disheartened with myself. My life before salvation was to prepare diligently above and beyond for all things asked of me. After I met Jesus, I never wanted to show up unprepared for anything. The trouble with this approach is that because of all the preparation, I began to lack spontaneity. I prepared with such a ferocity that despite pressing into prayer to present something pleasing to the Lord and a blessing for His people, I was less malleable for the Holy Spirit.

Often, when we put a lot of effort into something, we are reluctant to let it go. God is both a preparer and spontaneous, so please don't misunderstand me. I have learned that all the diligence in the Word of God and intimacy with the Holy Spirit with prayer are very important, but it's not about the product produced in written form (teaching, preaching, prophetic word, or exhortation). Our time in the Word and with the presence of the Holy Spirit has to do with knowing God and God knowing me, period. The diligence continues, but the stranglehold of rigidity around what is produced has been eliminated.

The Lord loves when we follow His lead. He has more interest in saving, healing, and doing miracles for people than we can even begin to imagine. His plans are perfect and for all the messages I have prepped and never given, I am grateful beyond measure. These messages remain personal for my own journey further into the heart of my heavenly Father.

To trust God and move with Him is to come into the rightful place of being evenly yoked with the Spirit of the living God and to become an active member in His divine plan. I cannot let my bones dry out. I have met so many pastors over the years who have lost their intimacy with God because they prepare so many messages and refuse to let them go for fear of losing control of the service or the people in the service. I crave being with God and listening to what He will say to me. I never grow weary in watching what He is doing. My joy in Him is complete. There is no greater love. When we learn this, we will be ready to let go of anything He asks of us.

By the end of that conference session, with the level of the presence of God in the room, there were perhaps six people left standing. All the others were resting in the glory of God in chairs or on the floor. Even the youth were touched mightily.

"I'd like for you all just to remain in receiving mode," I said. "Rest in the Lord and don't get up until you feel His presence lift off of you. Some of us really need refreshing while others are receiving deep physical, emotional, and spiritual healing."

From the back of the room, one of our new Agape ministry team members approached me.

"Hey, Jo, will you pray for my friend? He won't be here tomorrow. He's in the back." Tyler stretched out his arm and pointed.

In the very back of the room, another young man perched on a stool. He was wearing a button-down shirt, jeans, and brown-rimmed glasses. A quick smile revealed a very warm personality. I could sense the compassion for the lost in him.

"Hi, I'm Jo." I hugged him.

"Hi, I'm Kyle." He hugged me back.

"Hey, Kyle! Tyler came to get me to pray for you."

Tyler smiled and nodded toward his friend.

I continued, "So what do you need prayer for?"

"Anything God tells you is good with me," he said.

We laughed out loud.

"We'll see what the Lord has to say then." I smiled. "Holy Spirit, thank You that You are already here. I invite You to speak to Kyle, and help me, Lord, to have ears to hear and eyes to see what You're doing so that he will be mightily encouraged by You." I saw flashes of Africa and heard the Holy Spirit say, *You have a Reinhard Bonnke anointing!*

At those words the power of the Holy Spirit struck Kyle with such force he flipped off the stool and onto his stomach on the floor. The power of the Lord was so strong on his body that he was vibrating and moving almost in a circle. Tyler kept his phone near to record the prophetic word so Kyle would have it later.

For those of you who have never heard of Reinhard Bonnke, he lived the majority of his life focused on bringing Christ to the nation of Africa through the ministry he founded, Christ for All Nations. Seventy-nine million people came to Christ under the term of his directorship, and his successor, Daniel Kolenda, is continuing the legacy today. It is not unusual for more than a million and a half people to come to their crusades seeking a touch from Jesus from all across Zimbabwe to Nigeria.

"You are going to Tanzania!" I blurted before I had time to think. "Even this year!" The word was lengthy, and the Lord told me beautiful things of Kyle's dedication, faithfulness, and diligence. He told me of his family. The Lord is personal, and when He comes to bless His beloved ones through ordinary people like me and like you, being able to relay His love to someone is priceless.

Months after the conference, I received a video on Facebook Messenger. There was Kyle standing in the middle of a village in Africa. My heart beat faster while I listened.

"Jo Moody, I just want to thank you for prophesying and praying over me in Oklahoma. So much of what the Lord told you to tell me has already come true, and because of that I have had so much faith and courage on this trip. I wanted to tell you that when you said I was going to Tanzania that I thought you were nuts because I was not going to Tanzania. My trip was planned for Kenya. But guess where I am standing? Yep, Tanzania! We got rerouted here, and because of that word I knew it was right! Thank you so much for investing for me and for praying for me!"

I wish I had sent him a video of me laughing at the faithfulness of God to do such a tremendous thing through fallible people. In the next few days I would discover that more than 150,000 people came to Christ in three weeks, and many were healed as Kyle and his team led crusades. I also found out Kyle graduated from Christ For All Nations, and the team he was with was organized through Christ For All Nations, Reinhard Bonnke and Daniel Kolenda's ministry.

There is no one like our God. Psalm 73:25-26 says, *"Whom have I in heaven but you? I desire you more than anything on earth. My health may fail, and my spirit may grow weak, but God remains the strength of my heart; he is mine forever."*

To be able to walk with God in an intimate friendship and know that He is for you is a lifelong discovery process. Won't you believe Him even for this moment that your life was purposed for extraordinary divine partnership with the Holy Spirit?

What's Next Activation

— Prayer —

Lord, even the father with the demonized son had difficulty believing Jesus just before Jesus rebuked the demon and healed the boy. Right now, I pray You would have mercy on me and help my unbelief, Father. Jesus, Your Word promises that we would do even greater things than You did, and You raised the dead. You know me, You are familiar with all my ways and all my doubts. I choose to give You everything that hinders me now and trust that You will use me as I learn to risk praying for others and practice listening to You. I will release the words I believe You are giving to me, and I will not back up even when I might miss one. You built me to hear You and to change the lives of those around me by the presence of Your Holy Spirit. So, come, Holy Spirit, and fill me to overflowing that I will be the answer to someone's prayers. Thank You, Jesus.

Give It Away

Ask the Holy Spirit what you are to do with what you have learned from this chapter. I'm praying for you. Step out and risk. Practice with Him. He is your greatest cheerleader! I am your second cheerleader. You can do it. Christ is strengthening you at this very moment. Pray, "Lord, help my unbelief!" Your tiny "yes" has the Creator of the universe behind it!

11

The Unexpected

MAYBE FEAR IS GOD'S WAY OF SAYING,
"PAY ATTENTION, THIS COULD BE FUN."

CRAIG FERGUSON

In the first few years of ministry and traveling to Europe, I returned many times to the same cities and churches. Building the expanding family of Christ unified in a mission of love is, I believe, part of the riches of the inheritance that Jesus released to us and intercedes for us to fulfill. In Luke 8:18-21 Jesus is with a large crowd when His mother and brothers show up outside and begin calling for Him. Those around Jesus report that His family is outside. Jesus then remarks that His family are those who hear the Word of God and obey it. I know that Jesus loved His family of origin, but He also had His origin first in God the Father. He did the will of the Father.

Relationship with the Father, Son, and Holy Spirit is incredible and introducing others to the vibrancy held within the triune Godhead has no equal. We all come together in Him. He gives us supernatural kinship different from our family of origin.

As you've been reading, I pray you've begun to discover that the Holy Spirit is an adventurer, and life in Him is never lacking exhilaration. And yet, bringing the awareness of the depth of the Father's love and the fulfillment of what Jesus gave to us through the Holy Spirit is not without challenge. Some of my favorite recollections are introducing the Holy Spirit to churches, staff, and laypeople who have grown up with a love for God but have not previously had any relationship with the Holy Spirit. God's words and timing are personal, and perfect, for each person as He is building His family.

It was a crisp and overcast spring day in a suburb of London. I was excited to walk to the church, as we had not been to this particular church before. Six of our Agape ministry team and I walked the brick pathway through the neighborhood, past the vicarage, and onto the main street that housed the beautiful Anglican church at the end of the road.

"Can you believe most of these houses were built in the late eighteen hundreds and early nineteen hundreds? They have buildings all over the UK older than America!" I said. "Wild!"

"I like these brick sidewalks and all the gardens—so English," Michelle said.

Everyone smiled at everyone else. We would walk this route multiple times a day when we ministered here in St Alban's, and we loved every moment of it—even in the sleeting rain or freezing cold.

Once we went up the brick steps and into the warm lobby of the church, we shed our jackets and headed to the beautiful main sanctuary. Its high roofline and dark wood-beamed ceiling was framed in multicolored stained-glass windows. It was breathtaking. A clean, stark white linen draped the altar, and just at the base of the stairs leading up to the altar we gathered as a team. This was a holy place, and the peace of the Lord was present. Although the sanctuary was gorgeous and indeed a holy place, we were gathered together that morning for a staff team training and not a formal church service.

My dear friend, the vicar, Stephen, introduced us all around to his staff and team. Stephen and his wife, Lucy, have been in a love affair with the Holy Spirit for more than twenty-five years. He is a patient and loving man, and his heart's desire is to see the whole of the Anglican community have ongoing fellowship with the Holy Spirit to see revival come to the nation. We became fast friends on a Brazil trip earlier that same year, and when he asked if I would come to teach his staff, lay ministry team, and church members, I could not wait to join what the Lord had already begun.

With a trolley laden with tea, coffee, and cakes and the chairs circled up, we sat together. Great tea and abundant sarcasm abound in England, and for both of these reasons, I feel it is my second home.

As tea was consumed, worship began. We turned our attention to focus on God alone. Worship led to gratitude and spontaneous prayer.

Although some of Stephen's staff team were not quite sure what they had signed up for with our visiting American team, they endured for the moment. Many had never experienced the presence of the Holy Spirit. Their faces reflected uncertainty.

"Hey, everyone!" I smiled. "We are grateful for time with you this morning. I know you're all busy and Stephen has rallied you here perhaps without providing a ton of background of exactly what we are doing together. We are here to bless you, encourage you, and hopefully help you to move together in greater unity with less wasted time, energy, and misunderstanding."

A few people's mouths turned up at the corners. It became obvious that a speck of hope was felt by most.

I continued, "My background training is in executive coaching, human resources, leadership development, and team building. All of these areas are a passion of my life. When we intentionally invest in leaders, the Church begins to change. I know the Lord is building His Church as one Kingdom family without boundaries, denominational bias, gender, racial, or socioeconomic division. Whenever teams are assembled, my expectation—as well as the expectation of our Agape ministry team—is endless. We witness transformation through unity again and again. No matter what your experiences, the Lord is doing a new thing today. Are we in agreement to give things a try and see what happens?"

All around the circle, most began to nod. Still a few of the staff and team members had doubt circling overhead like a vulture. I smiled at them individually. Love and acceptance, meeting a person right where they are in the moment, allows the door to revelation to crack open within hearts. With some doors wide open and others cracked only enough for a vapor of new thought to enter, we plowed into the material.

The morning passed by like a bullet train. The team discovered personal values, individual learning, communication styles, and best practices for team unity based on the information collected. Even in the midst of a time spent with analytical data, the Holy Spirit was present. Oftentimes, I have found a tendency within certain groups of people to compartmentalize and separate the Holy Spirit from activities that might not feel overtly spiritual. I used to do that very thing until I began yielding even my compartmentalized notions to the Lord and asking Him to speak through whatever means He desires. Now I watch the Lord reach everyone—even the most analytical among us. Just because every person does not fall over under the weighty presence of God doesn't mean God is not speaking to them, touching them, or using them in mighty ways. The simple guide is this: Just don't resist God. Be open in heart, mind, and body. Give Him permission to do what He wants.

All of this brings me back to the moment we began to close the training meeting. The Lord had truly done marvelous things. I witnessed several people I knew well that had a history of disunity with one another—come to an understanding of why they had not been able to see eye to eye in the past. They now had factual data and ways to communicate that was not based solely on feelings. The time was well spent, and joy was evident in even the most tight-lipped starters as we shared a takeaway moment around the room.

"Everyone, we are going to wrap it up," I began. "I'm incredibly thankful to God for what He's done today but we are not finished quite yet. If you'll come back to your spots in the circle, I'd like to pray again and ask the Lord for prophetic words for our Agape team to share with each one of you."

Two in particular on the staff team became as tight-lipped as an afterthought but obliged the request to move into the circle. I looked up at our amazing Agape team, and they smiled. We had been here before with many teams.

"Holy Spirit, thank You that You are our very present help in times of trouble or unrest. You are the author and finisher of our faith, Lord Jesus. You have plans to prosper us and not to harm us, to give us a future and a hope. Come and make Your presence known to your sons and daughters that they may be mightily encouraged and further propelled into the destiny You have for them. All for Your glory and Your Name. Amen."

With that, our team moved around the circle and laid hands on each staff member. They spoke in hushed tones and released the love of the Father and prophetic words of encouragement over each one. I stepped over to the second person next to me. Alex's head was bent forward, and he had been one of the two tight-lipped team members. I had a strong impression from the Holy Spirit that this man was a composer and score writer for movies and television series. I had no idea if that was right, but the impression came like a movie running across my mind as I saw Alex in a studio creating these beautiful orchestrations. I leaned into his right ear.

"Alex, I know you are uncomfortable with all this Holy Spirit stuff, but I want to share something with you that I believe the Lord is showing me. If I am wrong, I will apologize, but if this is correct, I pray your heart will know the plans of the Lord in your life will be fulfilled if you simply trust Him."

His head remained bent.

I shared the prophetic impression and told him I believed he would be creating movie scores for major film and television projects in great recording studios among the best musicians.

Alex's head jerked upright, and he looked me square in the face. "How could you know that?!" His eyes spilled over with tears. "That's my dream. I am a composer."

"Because that is a gift from the Lord for some of your life's work, and the Lord wants you to know He has not forgotten your dream." I squeezed his shoulder.

Alex is an incredibly analytical man. He was having trouble comprehending the supernatural presence of the Lord through ordinary people.

I prayed over him and moved to the next person the Lord highlighted to me.

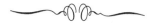

Later that evening at another public meeting in the church, Alex was playing keyboards as part of the worship team. I smiled at the prophetic word from the morning. During the teaching, I shared with everyone that I used to limit the Lord particularly by doubting claims of people finding gemstones on the floor or jewels appearing out of thin air during prayer time—until it happened to me. I could almost feel Alex's lips purse behind me, but he is far too polite for that when he is on the altar for worship.

"Listen, everyone." I looked around at the church filled to capacity and launched into a testimony. "A few years ago, I was gathered at a ministry event in America, and close to fifteen of us gathered in a circle to pray with a precious woman with fourth-stage terminal cancer. As we were praying, I witnessed with my eyes wide open, a gemstone popping out in midair right next to a woman's left ear. It dropped with a small plop onto the brown leather shoe of the woman next to her. Bouncing off the toe area of her left foot, it landed directly in front of my friend Lauren.

"'Aha! That's mine!' Lauren blurted. 'I have been praying for this!' She bent over and scooped up the small diamond-looking gem and put it into her pocket without stopping her prayers for the woman with cancer.

"I was incredulous. I jerked my attention back to praying but my mind turned over and over what I had just witnessed. We were attending a Voice of the Prophets conference on the East Coast of America. Throughout the public meetings with Mahesh Chavda, Dr. Randy Clark, and others, my friends and teammates began finding gemstones all over the floor. My mind still could not comprehend what was happening. I had no grid for this extravagance, so I didn't participate. I remained a confused observer instead of one engaged with childlike faith.

"On the last night of the conference I prayed, 'Lord, this outpouring is confusing to me. I don't understand the point of any of it, but my friends are having a blast finding these jewels. If this is all from You, I would love to be able to find one too before this conference ends in a few minutes.' I'd like to tell you I heard the audible voice of God in response but that did not happen. I heard and felt nothing. Instead, my friends continued to pick up many more stones until the very last moment. My meager last-minute hunt yielded nothing but threads and sparkly particles in the carpet beneath our feet. The last worship song played, and prayer ended the conference. The glory of God had been so prevalent throughout the conference and yet, I was focused on what I did not have.

"'Sorry you didn't find any, Jo. I could give you one of mine,' Lauren said. She opened up her wallet, and I peered inside. There were more than a dozen gemstones, and several looked to be over a carat in size. I turned into a three-year-old in my mind. *I want my own jewels, Lord. What a walking contradiction I am.* I felt ridiculous having this immature reaction after I had such doubt about the manifestation even being God. As I moved across the conference floor toward the exit, I continued to wrestle with the whole point of the gemstone outpouring while others simply enjoyed the supernatural moment.

"I walked out of the conference through one set of double doors and felt a sudden urge to stop. The Holy Spirit nudged me to look down. The crowd surged around us like water around a rock. It was a gathering of thousands. I looked down and there on the floor were two very tiny pale-pink gemstones. Stunned, I picked them up.

"'Ha-ha! I knew you'd find some!' Lauren and Michelle said almost in unison.

"I held the tiny stones in my hand and marveled at the huge number of facets within each one. The direct light overhead danced off of them in incredible brightness despite their small size. They were beautiful. I spoke to the Lord in my heart. *Lord, thank You so much! I am truly grateful but why are they so tiny?*

"I heard loud and clear from the Holy Spirit: *My love, by the measure of your faith do you receive.* What a teaching moment for me. God gives abundantly and when we join our faith to His promises there is always more. When we choose to remain in doubt, our lack of faith can hinder what the Lord has planned to release—in a moment and throughout our lives.

"Later that night in the hotel I prayed again for clarity about why the gemstones appear. I read in Psalm 115:3 the Lord God Almighty can manifest any way He chooses. I'm not even sure why I wrestled so much with the jewels even after I have seen the Lord do many miracles and healings in people's bodies. Weird, I know. I was reminded God appeared to Moses in a burning bush and it didn't burn up. A pillar of cloud by day and a fire pillar at night appeared in the wilderness to guide the children of Israel out of the land of Goshen through the Nile Delta in Egypt in order to enter the promised land. That is bizarre. Maybe a fluke. A one-time cloud in the daytime and a pillar of fire in the night sky is plausible, but these pillars appeared over and over again, and according to many scholars, the Israelites were led by these reappearing supernatural clouds for 38 years until they reached the promised land.

"The Word of God is full of unexplainable supernatural manifestations of God. The Lord loves to give good gifts to His children, and sometimes they seem strange. Okay, let's face it, much of the time they seem strange with our natural and finite brains. But the Lord is God and He dwells in unapproachable light. His ways are higher, and His Spirit cannot be contained. His goodness and faithfulness to bless our lives is immeasurable.

"I had limited God that day. I put His supernatural manifestations into parameters. Let's call it a box because that is what it is. My lack of acceptance of the way the Lord expressed the supernatural in this way didn't make sense to my natural mind and it caused my faith to falter. I wasn't even aware I had formed the box around God because I have seen so many miracles. The jewels popping out of midair was a stretch for me because it was new. Yet, it happened, and I believe now that the Lord creates these manifestations to cause us to wonder. 'A sign that makes you wonder.' That's what Bill Johnson says. Truly these signs are meant to make us wonder about the majesty and magnificence of God. The manifestations of God's supernatural power, authority, and creativity are not meant to be signs that cause you shut down. They are in invitation to know Him in greater ways.

"With all of this said, First John 4:1 speaks to us about testing the spirits as many have been deceived. Practicing discernment, aligning supernatural manifestations with the Word of God and His holy character and nature is vastly important when supernatural manifestations happen around you outside of your comprehension. Don't throw the baby out with the bathwater. I hope you have that idiom here in England! Seek the Lord above all else and everything will be added unto you including wisdom, revelation, and understanding. First John 2:27 tells us the Holy Spirit teaches us all things. Pray, study the Word, ask the Holy Spirit for revelation. Trust Jesus to give you understanding."

At the end of sharing the last part of the testimony, we prayed for most of the church who came forward, and many were healed of diseases and infirmities while others asked for prayer to overcome unbelief. One of those was Alex. He made a beeline for me and shared his heart with me while his eyes flooded with tears.

"Jo, I do want to have faith for this kind of thing. Since we left the worship area and I sat down, I have even been looking around on the floor as you spoke in case the Lord wanted to put some jewels there for me to find. All I found was this black small stone and a stray button, but I don't think that's God."

I smiled and hugged him.

He had so much faith. What a different young man than the one I met earlier that morning. One moment in the presence of the Holy Spirit through a prophetic word changes a lifetime of hurt and lack of perspective about Jesus and His plans for your life.

"Father, I pray for Alex now. You do desire to fulfill his destiny and release miracles to him and through him. Lord, if he wants to see supernatural gems, I pray You would do even more than that simply because You love him so much." I hugged him once more and watched him walk away.

The following morning, I woke up before 5:00 a.m. and went to my knees. I began praying and asking the Lord to move powerfully through signs, wonders, and miracles in all three of the Sunday morning services. I asked for Jesus to encounter those in fear and doubt with His radical love. I worshiped the Lord and rested in the richness of His presence.

Stand up and look on the bed.

It was a thought out of nowhere and not in context with what I was doing. I knew it was the Holy Spirit. I stood up and looked to my left. There on the queen bed comforter cover was a gemstone. Bright and shining, reflecting the morning light in blinding brilliance. *This is for Alex.*

Now it was my turn to cry. *Lord, how great You are! Thank You!*

We walked down the brick pathway to the church a few hours later. I kept God's treasure for Alex in a tiny bag inside my wallet, and I couldn't wait to tell him the story. Before our team prayer gathering, I entered the quiet sanctuary and found Alex at the sound booth checking levels of various channels on the mixer and changing batteries in the mic headsets.

"Hi, Alex!"

"Hey, Jo! You okay?" He looked up and smiled.

"I'm great. I have something for you." I reached into my bag and extracted the tiny clear pouch. I handed it to him.

"What! Is this what I think it is? No way!" He looked up at me and down again at the bag. The jewel sparkled inside the clear plastic as I shared my morning prayer time events. Fresh tears appeared in Alex's eyes. "I just can't believe God said this was for me. Can I tell you something else?"

I nodded.

"I came to work here part time even after I had applied for the full-time worship leader position and didn't get it. I have not felt good about myself since then. Even though I know we hired the right worship leader, I still couldn't get the rejection out of my head. I am grateful to work here, but my life is more than doing sound tech and playing keys in the services."

"I am glad you shared that with me. Our Father in Heaven has limitless love, acceptance, and provision for you. Let's pray." I put one hand on his shoulder and led him through a prayer to break the power of rejection from his life.

When the prayer was finished and the presence of the Lord's love engulfed Alex, he was overcome with joy. "I seriously thought you guys were a bit dodgy when I met you, but now, I am gobsmacked at what God has done for me."

"I don't know what 'gobsmacked' is, Alex, but I love the word and you. Here is to your newfound friendship with Jesus and fulfilling your dream of composing. May the favor of God be on you and all doors open for you to use your gifts for His glory."

A short time later, I received word that Alex had left his support role in the church to concentrate on music composition and production full-time from his home studio. His wife picked up more hours in her job while Alex pursued what they both believed was the calling of his life with faith to believe the Lord would make a way for them as they pursued Him above everything else. We enter the road to our true destiny when we experience total transformation through a personal touch from God.

The following year on my return to England, Alex was already hired to create the music score for films and several television series. He was having the time of his life creating beautiful music in partnership with the Holy Spirit and came to tell me how his life and family had changed. They welcomed another baby, and financially things were going well. His wife eventually left her job to stay home full time with their young children, now numbering three.

Six months ago, I saw Alex's post on social media. The photo was taken in front of Abbey Road Studios in downtown London where the iconic Beatles album was recorded. Alex was there recording with outstanding London musicians despite each musician recording their parts separately during the pandemic. It just shows that even a worldwide pandemic cannot stop what God ordains to happen. The caption on Alex's post said, "Dreams come true."

"Good for you, Alex!" I said aloud in my office.

God's dream in Alex has come true and when each of us matches our faith with God's destiny plan through prayer and perseverance, there is always more.

What's Next Activation

— Prayer —

Lord, if I have put You in a box because of my lack of understanding of Your majesty and glory, forgive me. When I have made You too small or feared You will not help me with the dreams I have, I am sorry. Holy Spirit, in the Name of Jesus, remove my limited thinking about You and what is possible in my life through You. I surrender my dreams to You now. Show me what hinders my faith to believe my dreams will come true—even the dreams I shelved long ago. Help me to match my faith with Your dream for my life. Give me boldness to risk seeking You first and daring to believe that You will add everything else I need to my life. Even when I don't understand, I will come back to Your Word, inviting

*Your Spirit to teach me wisdom in my innermost places.
I desire fellowship with You and revelation for all that
You are. Change my heart, O God, and let me be true
to all You have destined me to be. Give me action steps
to match my faith and may I grow in wisdom and favor
with You and others. Open doors that nobody can shut.
Use me for Your glorious Kingdom expansion. Amen.*

Praying for the Baptism of the Holy Spirit

As a believer you were filled with the Holy Spirit when you gave your
life to Jesus. But if you have never been baptized in the fire of the Holy
Spirit, I encourage you to pray this prayer:

*Lord Jesus, I believe You are Lord and King of the uni-
verse and You are Lord and King of my life. You gave
us Your Holy Spirit so that we would be Your light and
healing love upon this earth. I ask now in Your Name
for the fullness of the power of Your Holy Spirit to come
and baptize me with fire as the disciples experienced at
Pentecost. Come, Holy Spirit. I welcome You to touch
my life and empower me for the glory of God!*

Give It Away

I am always reminded by the Lord that we cannot give away what we don't have. Where has God increased your faith through Alex's story? Is there someone around you who has a narrow view of God? Perhaps they cannot fathom that the Lord would move on their behalf with manifestations of supernatural proportion. Maybe those people are in your own family or workplace. Ask the Holy Spirit what is the one thing you can do this week to allow you to give away what you have received through Him by faith. Ask Him to bless another's life with your simple prayers. Listen and watch for the nudge from the Holy Spirit. For those around you who have never experienced the Holy Spirit, ask if they are willing to allow you to simply pray for their introduction to Him. Lay your hands on their hands or shoulder and ask the Holy Spirit to come. Be patient but persistent.

I used to ask the Lord to manifest with a display of gold all over a person's hands or chest when we were praying for them. I know we don't need an outward manifestation of God to know He is there, but after seeing the trajectory of Alex's life, I pray you hear my heart here. I have seen thousands of people covered in a gold-like sheen so visible that they look like someone poured Christmas glitter on their skin. I usually tell them to go into the bathroom and wash their hands to see what happens. Charging back incredulously, they exclaim, "It doesn't wash off!" I usually respond with something like this: "In time, it will fade as the level of the anointing on you lifts off. Right now, the Lord is touching you powerfully, and He just wants you to know He's here and He's for you."

Go out and pray for at least one person in your increased faith this week. Watch the Lord move simply because He loves to bless every attempt we make to do what He has asked. I am praying for you. For those of you a bit more courageous, ask the Holy Spirit to manifest in signs and wonders and miracles right in front of your eyes as you pray for the one in front of you. Expect the Lord to show up and show His glory. There is no better life.

12

When Things Don't Make Sense

TRUST IN THE LORD WITH ALL YOUR HEART
AND LEAN NOT ON YOUR OWN UNDERSTANDING;
IN ALL YOUR WAYS SUBMIT TO HIM AND HE
WILL MAKE YOUR PATHS STRAIGHT.

PROVERBS 3:5-6 NIV

I was praying early one morning and pondering the tension of living in the supernatural promises of God. I see thousands of healings and miracles, and believe me, I am beyond grateful for all the things the Lord does. Here I am trying to inspire you to link arms with Jesus and live the amazing life you were born to live in Him, but I would be remiss if I didn't mention the challenges we face when things don't go as planned—the moments when we pray, inspired by the Holy Spirit, and the healing does not come. The days we have the faith to speak to ten mountains and make them move, and for some reason even a little molehill will not budge. How about this one? We pray for a miracle; a person receives that miracle and then loses their healing a few days or weeks later. The confusion, doubt, and disappointment caused by these scenarios is real and very challenging.

The natural world we live in demands answers. We are rife with information at our fingertips. If you try to decipher anything on almost any topic you can think of and you're still perplexed, there will be hundreds of others online to give you their opinions and solutions. God is not Google. He is majestic, divine, and holy. When healings or miracles don't manifest as we believe they should, we have one place to land our conclusions. God is in charge, not us. I realize that was quite possibly not the answer you were looking for. I wish I could apologize, but it is the truth.

Several years ago, many of our Agape Freedom Fighter's ministry team prayed for a man about forty years of age suffering with advanced stages of pancreatic cancer. When he was brought to us, he had a fever of 103 degrees Fahrenheit and had to be carried into the prayer room on a stretcher. The Lord moved quickly, and in a matter of minutes, the man had no fever, no pain in his body, and exclaimed how incredible he felt.

"I'm going home to finish doing the crown molding I was installing before I got sick," he said and walked out of the room with a bounce in his step.

I heard he worked on his house for a week straight with no symptoms of any sickness. Glory to God! After that week, his symptoms came back with a vengeance. Over the weeks ahead this cycle would repeat many times. We prayed, and he would have no manifestation of illness, even returning to the doctor to find his test results improving.

One day, I got a call asking if I would make a trip to the couple's house.

Lord, what would you have me do? I prayed.

Child, go. I want you to bless him, bless his wife and his family. This will be difficult for you, but I love you. I love this son and his family. Do not look at what your eyes see. Keep your eyes on Me and your hand in Mine. All at once, I saw Jesus' nail-scarred hands take my hand and lead me forward.

I was in tears before I arrived at their home.

His wife greeted me at the door with red-rimmed eyes and her mouth slack. She looked numb and overwrought at the same time.

I folded her into my arms and prayed. *Father, release Your love over Your beloved daughter. Jesus, be her peace. Holy Spirit, come and surround this family.*

She led me upstairs to their bedroom.

I barely recognized the withered and unconscious man lying in the huge bed. Six short weeks had passed since our first prayer and less than two weeks from the last meeting. *Lord, I need help. I know I heard prophetic words for his destiny every time we prayed with him. I released those words over him and over his wife, and now he is dying. I don't understand.* My eyes filled with tears, but I tried to take a deep breath, so I could pray aloud. I didn't know what to pray anymore.

Dearest Joanne, I am the way, I am the truth, I am the life. Anyone who believes in Me will not perish but have everlasting life. You did what I asked and though you do not understand in this moment, I am love. You are here as My love.

The Lord's presence in the room was palpable. And in that moment, I stopped thinking about how confusing all of this was. Instead, as this dying man's wife stood next to me weeping, I opened my *Passion Translation* Bible to Matthew 6:9-13 and prayed the prayer that Jesus taught us all.

Our Beloved Father, dwelling in the heavenly realms, may the glory of your name be the center on which our lives turn. Manifest your kingdom realm, and cause your every purpose to be fulfilled on earth, just as it is in heaven. We acknowledge you as our Provider of all we need each day. Forgive us the wrongs we have done as we ourselves release forgiveness to those who have wronged us. Rescue us every time we face tribulation and set us free from evil. For you are the King who rules with power and glory forever. Amen.

With the guidance of the Holy Spirit, I prayed a final prayer.

Lord, release Your beloved son from torment and pain and usher him into the fullness of Your love-light for all eternity.

The Bible says we live in a holy tension. Paul emphasized that point in Philippians 1:21 (ESV): *"For me to live is Christ, and to die is gain."* Do you read that verse and say, "Huh?" Paul makes a point to speak of life and death in the same sentence, which has often caused me to ponder how I filter challenging situations when the outcome did not go as I presumed it would. In Paul's brief sentence in Philippians 1:21, he lays out the paradox of our life in Christ.

Jesus is alive in us and, therefore, when we are truly living according to this verse and the supernatural promises of God, our lives are a manifestation of Christ's glory, yet our death is our ultimate gift—to live forever in the glory realm with our creator, God. Therein lies the tension of our earthly lives. Some believers focus entirely on getting to Heaven without adopting the assignment here to advance the Kingdom through divine partnership with the Holy Spirit. Others of us desire to fulfill our destiny and jump in with both feet to the things of the supernatural because we understand as we live in Jesus, the world sees and knows He is alive! But when life in the supernatural leads to death in the natural, we are perplexed.

Read Philippians 1:21 again. We cannot give into our human understanding of God's sovereignty. We must learn to navigate the tension of living in the *now* and the *not yet*. The Kingdom has *come* upon us, and it is *coming* upon us. We are the glory of Jesus Christ, and His life in us produces great things. And yet when we die, it will be His perfect completed mission that we are unified in glorious eternity with our Father in Heaven. Let that be our understanding as we look at a few more things concerning confusion and loss within our supernatural assignments.

When we have done all the Lord asks and a person's miracle is lost— or their healing never fully manifests despite accurate prophetic words and a powerful display of the presence of God—it is devastating. Many people will stop partnering with the Lord in the supernatural after experiencing this level of heartbreak. It is tempting, when things get difficult, to throw in the towel and declare, "Game over." Don't do it.

Analyzing and brooding over what was lost is a product of fear and grief. When the human mind looks for solutions outside of divine encounter, it is the response to feeling out of control. With that said, I do believe there is opportunity for us to grow and mature as we sit with the Lord and ask Him what He has to say about the situation that has us perplexed and overwrought.

Healings and miracles are often lost for a myriad of reasons. When I was healed, Richard, the man who prayed for me, told me this:

"Listen, Joanne. That thing (spirit of affliction and pain) has been on you a long time. It is going to try and come back. You have to imagine it is a snake that is trying to bite you. If any pain returns, tell it, 'No! Get out in the Name of Jesus!'"

I admit I thought that advice was nuts because I had no symptoms after I was healed. But not twenty-four hours later, I felt pain like a knife stabbing me through my pelvis—the same pain that had plagued me for almost fifteen years. I gasped. The pain was sharp and piercing, taking my breath away.

Then I remembered Richard's words about the pain trying to return.

If this is a snake, Lord, I have to respond.

"No! Get out in the Name of Jesus!" I yelled.

The pain instantly evaporated. I was incredulous.

This same process went on daily, and each time the pain came, it was less intense. Then everything shifted toward the end of the second week. By that time, I was fully aware of the spiritual battle I was in. Jesus gave me victory and as long as I did not agree with the spirit of affliction trying to gain access to me again, it would grow weary and leave. At the end of the second week, the pain came again, but it was very mild.

"I told you to get out in the Name of Jesus!" I said. "I am healed! Now don't come back!"

The pain never returned, and it has been eight years. Glory, hallelujah. I had learned to contend. Maybe that is new for you. It certainly was for me. Let's remember that this world is fallen, satan roams around looking for people to devour (see 1 Pet. 5:8), and we are the representatives of Jesus' victorious triumph over death, so we are his target. We are in a supernatural battle, yet Jesus is our ever-present help in times of trouble (see Ps. 46:1) We are not contending to obtain the victory; rather, through contending we are drawing upon the perfect atonement—Jesus' complete victory over the enemy that was won on the cross.

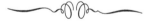

I've spoken much throughout this book about our identity in Christ, agreeing that we are who He says we are is the most important shift that must take place in our hearts in order to partner with God to do His works. Knowing and standing upon our identity in Christ and embracing His perfect flawless position as God is the best place to contend to maintain healing. The more secure we are in Jesus, the less space the enemy has to bring harassment.

I have also learned from the Lord that some healings are lost due to a person's environment. I have seen people get out of wheelchairs only to lose their healing months later as they became saturated by their verbally abusive family member's words. The power of life and death is in the tongue (see Prov. 18:21) and when we live with someone cursing us each day, it can be challenging to maintain our healing when we soak in and give agreement to their words. With this said, we must seek the Lord for His revelation and a new understanding of each situation that perplexes us. We must fight the urge to assume we know why a healing was lost or never fully manifested. Sometimes there is no explanation, and we must surrender our demand for an answer to the Lord in holy reverence and awe.

He is Lord and His will is perfect. God is supernatural, Yahweh, creator God. The Creator creates, molds, shapes, and morphs every single life according to what will glorify Him most. Romans 11:33 (ESV) says, *"Oh, the depth of the riches and wisdom and knowledge of God! How unsearchable are his judgments and how inscrutable his ways!"* Our role is to pray without ceasing with thanksgiving, to live in communion and divine unity with the Father, Son, and Holy Spirit. He alone has power over life and death, and we are His witnesses, His children whom He has chosen so that we would know and believe and understand He is who He says He is. There is and never will be any other God like Him (see Isa. 43:10-11).

What's Next Activation

— Prayer —

*Lord, I admit I often try to control the outcomes when
I become overwhelmed. You are the only one in control*

over all life and death. I release my fear to You, and I ask that You give me a laser focus on Your face. Reveal more of Yourself to me so when I pray over someone, and things do not go as I believe they should, I will not lose heart. You are victorious, Lord Jesus, and I surrender my preconceived notions or ideas about how You ought to move. I desire You. Not just Your gifts. Teach me all about You so that when trouble and disappointment come, I will look to You for comfort and wisdom. Apart from You, I can do nothing good.

Dive deeper. Now pray to the Lord in your own words about anything else that weighs you down. Pray with all of your heart. God our Father is drawing you close.

Dear reader, I am praying this for you. Please pray it aloud over yourself.

I have not stopped thanking God for you. I pray for you constantly, asking God, the glorious Father of our Lord Jesus Christ, to give you spiritual wisdom and insight so that you might grow in your knowledge of God. I pray that your hearts will be flooded with light so that you can understand the confident hope He has given to those He called—His holy people who are His rich and glorious inheritance. I also pray that you will understand the incredible greatness of God's power for us who believe Him. This is the same mighty power that raised Christ from the dead and seated Him in the place of honor at God's right hand in the heavenly world to come. God has put all things under the authority of Christ and has made Him Head over all things for the benefit of the

Church. And the Church is His body; it is made full and complete by Christ, who fills all things everywhere with Himself (see Ephesians 3:16-17).

Give It Away

Everyone will struggle in this world, yet we are ambassadors of Christ's love to bring hope in the storms and upheaval of planet earth. When you meet someone struggling amid confusion and grief, when God is mysterious and there are no clear answers to why their healing did not come, or even when a person was healed and lost their healing later, ask the Holy Spirit how to come alongside them. People need an encounter with Jesus, not worldly advice. The love of Christ is peace, hope, joy, goodness, patience, gentleness, kindness, and more. That is who you are. Release these attributes of the Holy Spirit as you stand with the hurting one in front of you. Invite the Holy Spirit to take over. Even in silence, He is at work. When we have no clear answers there is still a way forward. His Name is Jesus, and He will light the path for the afflicted one even when it doesn't make sense.[1]

NOTE

1. For any additional information on finding breakthrough for healing prayer or maintaining healing, I recommend my friends Craig Miller and Dr. Randy Clark's book called *Finding Victory When Healing Doesn't Happen* (Apostolic Network of Global Awakening, 2015).

13

The Altruistic Life

WE MAKE A LIVING BY WHAT WE GET,
WE MAKE A LIFE BY WHAT WE GIVE.

SIR WINSTON CHURCHILL

In my quiet time one morning I heard the Holy Spirit say, *Let your life be altruistic in every way.*

In case you need reminding like I did, *altruistic* means to be unselfishly concerned *for* or concerned *with* the welfare or well-being of others, often at great personal risk. To be generous and unselfish, benevolent, humanitarian, or charitable.

When the Lord speaks to me specifically, I will spend time in His Word, directed by what He's speaking about.

I'll ask you what He asked me: *Which person(s) in the Bible stand out to you as altruistic?* (I hope you have many examples coming to you. Write down any altruistic biblical characters that come to mind. You'll need those for our What's Next Activation at the end of the chapter.)

Here was my immediate response to the Lord's prompting: *You, Jesus, modeled an entire lifestyle of altruistic behavior.*

I felt the Holy Spirit respond, *Yes, I did. Now who else can you think of?*

I know I have said it before, but it bears repeating. First John 2:27 tells us that the Holy Spirit teaches us all things. I know He loves bringing revelation. Like a light bolt of lightning, the story of the good Samaritan popped into my head.

I opened to Luke 10:25-37 (NIV) and read.

On one occasion an expert in the law stood up to test Jesus. "Teacher," he asked, "what must I do to inherit eternal life?" "What is written in the Law?" he replied. "How do you read it?" He answered, "'Love the Lord your God with all your heart and with all your soul and with all your strength and with all your mind'; and, 'Love your neighbor as your-self.'" "You have answered correctly," Jesus replied. "Do this and you will live." But he wanted to justify himself, so he asked Jesus, "And who is my neighbor?" In reply Jesus said: "A man was going down from Jerusalem to Jericho, when he was attacked by robbers. They stripped him of his clothes, beat him and went away, leaving him half dead. A priest happened to be going down the same road, and when he saw the man, he passed by on the other side. So too, a Levite, when he came to the place and saw him, passed by on the other side. But a Samaritan, as he traveled, came where the man was; and when he saw him, he took pity on him. He went to him and bandaged his wounds, pouring on oil and wine. Then he put the man on his own donkey, brought him to an inn and took care of him. The next day he took out two denarii and gave them to the innkeeper. 'Look after him,' he said, 'and when I return, I will reimburse you for any extra expense you may have.' Which of these three do you think was a neighbor to the man who fell into the hands of robbers?" The expert in the law replied, "The one who had mercy on him." Jesus told him, "Go and do likewise."

There is so much we can focus on in this story from the motives of the lawyer to the incredible patience of Jesus. But, my focus for us is what we can learn from the Samaritan that will impact how we choose to live in Christ day to day. The lawyer in the parable is trying to set Jesus up, and Jesus points him back to the law just as He will point us back to His Word. The man answers correctly, but the position of his heart is corrupt. He doesn't fully embrace Jesus' answer and confirmation of the law—that in order to inherit eternal life, one must love

God first with everything in us—mind, body soul, strength—and love everyone else with equal passion, commitment, and intention. The lawyer is looking for a loophole, a way to wiggle out of the commandment to love with extravagance, no strings attached, and nothing held back. So, he asks Jesus, "How do you define neighbor?" As an answer, Jesus paints a detailed portrait of the life of one who lives committed to God and desires to fulfill their complete destiny.

Read Luke 10:25-37 once, more and let's gather some things we can take with us.

In this parable, the Samaritan's altruistic behavior is displayed through great courage and generosity to benefit another despite the inconveniences, barriers, obstacles, and danger. Altruism is showing great compassion and extending time, resources, and care. The Samaritan chose to provide for another's welfare with compassion. The Father gave us the ultimate example of this when He gave Jesus as the ransom for our lives (see John 3:16). Jesus said, *"There is no greater love than to lay down one's life for one's friends"* (John 15:13) and, *"Love your enemies! Do good to them. Lend to them without expecting to be repaid"* (Luke 6:35). Paul writes in Second Corinthians 9:6-7 that when we sow bountifully, we will reap bountifully. It is the generosity of the Lord to pour His extravagant love over us in increasing measure so that we may turn and do likewise to those around us. The altruistic life is the generous life filled with rich intimacy in Jesus to inspire you to join Him in every way.

I've spoken many times publicly about generosity that leaves a legacy. The altruistic life does just that because to live this way is only possible through the generosity of Jesus and the supernatural workings of the Holy Spirit through us.

When my son, Kian, was about seven years old, he had two little friends in the back seat of our car, and I had to drive them a short distance for a school field trip. Because I was a chronic pain patient and rarely able to do much for his school, this short outing was special for me. I could be with my son as he learned and contribute to their class. I tuned in to listen to the conversation my son was having with his two friends on the way home from the school event. They were laughing and changing topics as fast as popcorn popping. I smiled. It is good to be around childhood banter. They were so free.

As I approached an intersection, I saw a homeless man standing on the corner, holding a sign that said, "Please help. No home." I was focused on the boys in the back seat, but I prayed anyway. *What do you want me to do, Lord?* I felt compelled to stop and give the man some money. So I drove up, then rolled down my window, handed him the cash, and said, "God bless you."

"God bless you, ma'am," he replied with a toothless grin. "God bless you. Thank you."

The light turned green, and I accelerated the car. From the back seat I heard the small-framed, brown-eyed, brown-haired boy in the middle say to my son, "Hey, why'd your mom do that? My mom says don't ever give homeless people any money 'cause they just buy drugs and alcohol."

I looked at the three of them in the rear-view mirror as I drove, curious. Compassion overtook my son's face. He leaned forward in his navy-blue booster seat as far as his seat belt restraint would allow and looked right into the eyes of his friend next to him. "Well, we're Christians, and the Bible says we're supposed to love people and help them when they need something."

Okay, I admit it. I got choked up for a second.

Then a fiery little voice erupted from the back seat like a fastball out of right field. "Well, we're Jewish, so we don't do any of that stuff." My son's adorable, stocky, red-haired, freckly-faced friend had weighed in.

I had to stifle a laugh. I loved the honesty of these precious boys. Perspective is everything. Each child was speaking the truth of their own family, what they had learned and understood was true. But we, as Christ's holy ambassadors, are to live His truth. Matthew 5:16 (NASB) says, *"Let your light shine before people in such a way that they may see your good works, and glorify your Father who is in heaven."*

As I pulled into our neighborhood and dropped each boy at their own home, I prayed, *Please, Lord, help us all to love as You do and teach our children to do the same.*

Francis Du Toit, in the Mirror Bible, said this: *"The destiny of the Logos [the word of God] was not to be caged in a book or a doctrine but to be documented and unveiled in human form! Human life is the most articulate voice of Scripture. Jesus is God's language; mankind is his audience"* (Heb. 1:1-3).

No matter what these young boys are taught, they had witnessed love and heard my own son declare why we must be extravagant in giving it all away: Because we are Christians.

Isaiah 58:6-7 (ESV) portrays the altruistic life in a way that we can tangibly grasp as we make the decision to life for the legacy of Jesus: *"Is not this the fast that I choose: to loose the bonds of wickedness, to undo the straps of the yoke, to let the oppressed go free, and to break every yoke? Is it not to share your bread with the hungry and bring the homeless poor into your house and when you see the naked, to cover him, and not to hide yourself from your own flesh?"*

I've reworded it similarly to *The Message* and made the altruistic life into a list. I like lists.

- Fast your life.
- Free those wrongly accused.

- Lift the burdens of those who work for you or around you.

- Help the oppressed be set free.

- Remove the chains that bind people.

- Share your food with the hungry.

- Give shelter to those without homes.

- Give clothes to those who need them.

- Do not hide from relatives who need your help.

This is by no means an exhaustive list, but it gives us the heart of Jesus at a glance.

Micah 6:8 says, *"The Lord has told you what is good, and this is what he requires of you: to do what is right, to love mercy, and to walk humbly with your God."* Let's do that. Be people of justice for the oppressed and imprisoned, to extend mercy and compassion and in humility consider others better than ourselves.

As we take daily action to partner with the Holy Spirit, Isaiah 58:8-9 tells us what the Lord promises will occur. *"Do this and the lights will turn on, and your lives will turn around at once. Your righteousness will pave your way. The God of glory will secure your passage. Then when you pray, God will answer. You'll call out for help and I'll say, 'Here I am'"* (MSG).

What's Next Activation

Remember when I asked you to write down altruistic people from the Bible who came to mind? I encourage you to look at the virtues those biblical characters modeled and make a list of the virtues that capture your attention. Ask the Lord what He has to say about these altruistic virtues in regard to your own life. Here is a list of questions to prompt you, but I encourage you to speak and ask the Lord from your own heart.

— *Prayer* —

Lord, what are You teaching me through these virtues?

Write down what the Holy Spirit tells you.

Lord, show me how to express these virtues in my daily life.

Heavenly Father, what specific steps toward embracing an altruistic life are You asking of me now?

Father, You know my schedule, relationships, and my resources. You know what is needed in order for me to live like the good Samaritan. I ask for You to release everything I need in order to be Your blessing to the one in need. I ask for the wisdom, grace, and unity of Your Spirit as I risk everything to do what You have asked.

Give It Away

Our lives are not our own but bought with the very precious blood of Jesus. You have now read many accounts of partnering with God in the life of divinity you were designed for. You are His holy reflection, mirroring His love to the world. Reflecting on your What's Next Activation questions, now it's time to take action, not just once or even once a week. Move your action into your lifestyle with dedication and commitment. Even when it's hard. Even when you don't feel like it.

Ask the Lord to give you a divine appointment each day and accept His invitation. Take risks! Be bold in love so that the altruistic life of Christ in you is displayed for His glory and so that the spread of His eternal Kingdom continues without end. Don't stop. You were built for this and born for such a time as this. Come on, world changer, let's change the world! Jesus has great plans to prosper you, to give you continual hope and an unmatched future in the supernatural everyday life of those who believe.

14

God's Reflection

IF YOU CANNOT FEED A HUNDRED PEOPLE,
THEN FEED JUST ONE.

MOTHER TERESA

Jesus said to the disciples in Acts 1:8 (NIV), *"But you will receive power when the Holy Spirit comes on you; and you will be my witnesses in Jerusalem, and in all Judea and Samaria, and to the ends of the earth."* Jesus calls the disciples His witnesses, exhorting them to share the things they've seen and heard in His presence. In Matthew 28, we, as His followers are given the same commission. In this passage we are charged to live as His reflection being His disciples and making disciples by sharing His word and truth through testimonies of what we have experienced personally through His presence and His love.

Romans 10:14-17 in *The Message* says:

But how can people call for help if they don't know who to trust? And how can they know who to trust if they haven't heard of the One who can be trusted? And how can they hear if nobody tells them? And how is anyone going to tell them, unless someone is sent to do it? That's why Scripture exclaims, "A sight to take your breath away! Grand processions of people telling all the good things of God!" But not everybody is ready for this, ready to see and hear and act. Isaiah asked what we all ask at one time or another: "Does anyone care, God? Is anyone listening and believing a word of it?" The point is: Before you trust, you have to listen. But unless Christ's Word is preached, there's nothing to listen to.

"Faith comes by hearing, and hearing by the word of God" is the more common translation of Romans 10:17 (NKJV). One thing that I have learned, seen, and confirmed thousands of times over the last seven years is the power of the testimony of what God has done is a key to

faith for believers and unbelievers alike. For what the human mind would like to deny, the spirit within each of us confirms in enthusiastic agreement of the truth of the majesty, power, and authority of God. What was born in you and me before the beginning of time is an ability to respond to God.

Ephesians 1:4 speaks of how God predestined us even before the earth was formed to be adopted as His sons and daughters. He is the all-sufficient Creator—the very One to give us life and from the beginning of conception we are a spirit being connected to Yahweh, creator God.

Even my atheist friends are drawn to faith when testimonies of healing, deliverance, and miracles are shared. Almost always, they are the ones asking me to share what God is doing. It used to be puzzling to me that someone professing the denial of God's existence desires to hear what I have been doing with God. But I have experienced that God's spirit within them, while yet unclaimed for Jesus, craves the supernatural truth of God for everyone is born with that desire but some have buried it so deeply within that they are no longer aware. Testimonies of God's glorious nature and majestic power and love bring living water to those living without Him and even those professing He is not real. As they hear, there is a shift even if you and I cannot comprehend it in the moment. Seeds are sown! God's Word never returns void (see Isa. 55:11) and the testimony of Jesus is the spirit of prophecy announcing to all who hear that Jesus Christ is alive and very active in every life (see Rev. 19:10). Our lives must continue to grow as an open invitation for those in doubt, fear, and bondage to encounter Jesus' authentic love. No one is too far from the reach of God, and some of the most unlikely scenarios are created when we simply add our willingness to step into what the Holy Spirit is asking of us.

I have a friend, Ari, who has lived eight decades of submission and obedience to Christ. He has discipled thousands of men and rescued them from addictions and incarceration. He teaches them construction trades and employs them as he is able. Ari brings the hurting, rejected, and abandoned face-to-face with Jesus through his partnership with the Holy Spirit. With the guidance of Ari and the consistency of the Lord, orphan-hearted men find forgiveness. They encounter a father, friend, teacher, and champion defender. If you ask Ari who he is, he will tell you he is just a cowboy from Oakdale, California. I can tell you that in the ten years I have known him, he is far more than that.

I first laid eyes on him outside our mega church in Northern California a few months after I received my miracle healing. I had been having great difficulty from many of the elders and some congregants of our conservative church. My own healing and the subsequent healings that were breaking out all over the church had caused an uproar in our church that struggled believing in the gifts of the Holy Spirit. I had recently been told that I was no longer allowed to pray publicly.

"Hey, young lady, the Lord is doing powerful things through you!" Ari said in a rich baritone voice with his deep-blue eyes flashing, catching me in the parking lot one day.

"Hi! Uh, thanks. I'm not sure I'm the most popular person on the campus these days though. Have we met?" I said.

His mouth broke into a great grin that filled his face. "I know all about you and the way the Holy Spirit is moving through you. Don't you worry about what other people say. You just listen to the Lord. He's got great plans for you, and I'm praying for you." With a wink and quick hug, he walked off.

What an amazing man, Lord. Thank You for that encouragement.

I would later discover that Ari led Bible studies for men, and I learned bits and pieces of what the Lord did through his passionate love of Scripture and the presence of the Holy Spirit. I became friends with his beautiful wife, June, and saw them periodically over the years, even after the Lord released me from the mega church where I had been on staff. They have always prayed for me and supported our Agape Freedom Fighters ministry.

Fast-forward to mid-2020 when Ken, an Agape team member, told me that Ari had been diagnosed with cancer. We set up a Zoom call because of COVID restrictions, and the glory of the Lord was present. Ken laid hands on Ari as I prayed from the screen. Months went by, and I received an update from Ken that Ari now had advanced stages of cancer and was dealing with overwhelming pain. I remained undaunted despite the doctor's diagnoses. I know the Lord moves powerfully even in advanced stages of disease. Since Ari and June desired for us to come over and pray in person, I was delighted to be able to see them and pray for complete healing.

Kathi and I drove together and met Ken in Ari's driveway.

"Hey, Ken! Good to see you," I said. "How come there are toilets out here in the driveway?" I laughed.

He smiled. "Yeah, there are two of them out here. They have someone here installing all new ones since they just moved into this house a few months ago." Then he walked toward the front door.

We climbed up the stairs to a beaming June waiting just inside the open front door. After warm embraces she took us into the living room, and eventually Ari made his way from the bedroom to us.

"Hiya, Ari! It's so good to see you!" I said.

"Well, it's good to be seen," he replied. "I'm glad you guys could come. Thanks for making the time."

I continued. "You know we love you guys. It's an honor to come over here. So, what's happening? You want to tell me how you're doing before we start praying?" I am always the one who wants to get right to the healing and then sit around and laugh about life.

"Before you all pray for me, I have something else I want to ask you to do."

I could feel a Holy Spirit setup. "Sure thing. Name it."

"Hey, Brian, will you come out here?" Ari's eyes glowed in the merriment that I have seen often, just before the Lord does something powerful. He was sitting in a chair as June, her grown daughter, Ken, Kathi, and I stood around him.

A tall stocky man dressed in shorts, athletic shoes, and a black T-shirt soaked through with sweat walked into the room.

"Brian, these are my friends. This is Jo, Kathi, and Ken. If you'd let them, I would love for them to pray for you."

Brian's eyes widened and he looked like he wanted the floor to open up and swallow him whole.

"Hi, Brian!" I began. "If Ari wants us to pray for you, I hope you'll consider allowing us to do it. God healed me of almost fifteen years of nerve damage, thirteen surgeries, a near-death experience, and chronic twenty-four-seven pain. I was on seven different opiates, so if anyone understands pain, it is me. More importantly, Jesus heals today. You have really bad back pain, right?"

Brian looked from my face to Ari's, and Ari's face lit up like Christmas. "I didn't tell them anything, okay? This is Jesus they're listening to."

"Uh, yeah," Brian said. "I have terrible back pain. Hips too."

I looked at Ken and Kathi. Kathi nodded. When you pray with a team that runs as a family, there is a connection to the Holy Spirit where you just know the orchestrated invitation of the Lord to radically impact the life in front of you. It's an absolute joy to do this in partnership with God but also with each other. "Okay, if level ten is the worst pain anyone could have, what is your pain level?"

"It's eleven. My hips and feet too."

Kathi, Ken, and I could feel the weight of the trauma this man had endured physically, emotionally, and spiritually. "Would it be okay if we prayed for you?" I asked. "We all believe this is your time for freedom."

"What do I have to do?" He looked over at Ari's reassuring smile and nod.

"Just stand here...unless you'd rather sit."

"Uh, standing is okay, but if I close my eyes, I'll fall over. I can't keep my balance anymore because of the pain in my back and hips."

"Don't worry about that. Jesus is going to give you a makeover." Kathi, Ken, and I laughed.

"I'm so sweaty. I'm sorry. I didn't know this was going to happen over here." Brian looked about to bolt.

I looked over at Ari, who smiled and winked at me. I know this friend of mine. No matter his own illness, there was always a man who needed Jesus' touch around him, and until his last day he would be about our heavenly Father's business. Ari and June live by Matthew 25:40 (NIV): *"Truly I tell you, whatever you did for one of the least of these brothers and sisters of mine, you did for me."* Silently I thanked the Lord for bringing us to witness the miracle I could sense was about to take place.

Then I focused on Brian's eyes and looked deeply into his pain.

"Dude, listen. We pray for people in the streets in India and Cambodia, and we pray for bishops in the church in London. It doesn't matter to us at all. We just love who God loves, and that's you. Relax. Take a couple of deep breaths."

Brian smiled albeit weakly and sighed.

For the next thirty minutes, Kathi, Ken, and I listened to the Holy Spirit give us words of knowledge and words of wisdom into the life of Brian. The Lord showed us the weapons the enemy had used against him in childhood through abuse and fatherlessness and later addiction, homelessness, and violence. Each of these areas of pain was reframed and healed through the infinite love of the Father. All abuse and abandonment were introduced into the light of Jesus and every unworthy thought and cursing lie broken by the presence and power of the Holy Spirit. Brian's mind, heart, and soul healed in a moment, and from there the manifestation of pain, instability, and trauma left his back, hips, and feet. He wept, and we celebrated.

"I...I can't even believe this is happening to me," he stammered. "What? I don't have any pain, and I can close my eyes!" Then he squatted down and up with his eyes closed.

We shouted, "Yay Jesus!"

Ari laughed and said, "Jesus set you up."

I thought about that for a minute and realized how often Jesus sets people up. As we saw that day, the Lord sets us up while we are doing ordinary things like installing toilets. But sadly, sometimes the believers around hurting folks don't recognize the moment and step into the place of invitation to bring about the opportunity for the one bound up in pain and struggle to receive a miracle.

Next, Brian joined us in prayer for Ari as we taught him to lay his hands on Ari and listen with his heart to what the Lord was impressing him to pray for. In that moment, the former orphan became a son who turned into a prayer warrior. That's how it works in the Kingdom.

First John 4:7 is an important truth in Scripture to help understand what happened to Brian. The Word says, *"Beloved, let us love one another, for love is from God, and whoever loves had been born of*

God and knows God. Anyone who does not love does not **know** *God, because God is love"* (ESV). The Greek word used for *know* is *ango* and it means "recognize" or "take in." When a person believes they are less than desirable, their past sin is unforgiveable, or they have been beaten down through verbal and physical abuse, there is often an inability to absorb the love of God. Many healing ministers refer to this broken state as "an orphan spirit." The orphan spirit is not a demonic spirit you can cast out. Rather, it is a mindset that creates an identity crisis. The orphan spirit prevents the heart (mind, will, and emotions) of a person from taking in the love of the Father, therefore rendering a person feeling as if they are unwanted and without value.

Ari opened his life and his heart to Brian years before. Through that father-son relationship, Brian began to heal from the well of abandonment and abuse he suffered as a child. Trust was established. Although Brian believed in Jesus, he had not experienced the supernatural presence of the Holy Spirit. When we prayed for him, the Holy Spirit highlighted any other areas of deception or pain in Brian's mind and soul. As these areas were healed, the love of the Father poured over Brian and he could finally receive it. Brian absorbed the truth of the magnitude and power of God's divine and perfect love for him, just as First John 4:7 says. He recognized and took in God's love and gave it away as he prayed for Ari for the first time—not with human love but with the love of Jesus.

Ari and Jesus are quite a team. As we stood in the driveway before leaving for home, Ken let us know that Ari had rescued Brian from drugs and alcohol and taught him construction four years before. Brian was about to sit for his general contractor's license and had been sober and clean for more than three years. When Ari learned Brian's pain was worsening, and he was struggling to keep working, he decided that the day we were coming to pray for his cancer healing was the day that Brian would be healed. To love others the way Jesus loves us.

I am currently waiting to hear the news of Ari's healing confirmed with a clear PET scan, and as I wait, I thank the Lord that He is divine and mysterious. He includes us in this life of wonders and simply asks us to pray by faith with thanksgiving. Regardless of the outcome, He is always good, always on the throne, and more interested in the person being touched, healed, and delivered than we are.

What's Next Activation

— Prayer —

Heavenly Father, I come to You again for transformation. Remove the next layer of indifference or even busyness that would cause me not to make time for Your Holy Spirit setups. Help me see those around me the way You do, and the way Ari does. In my life, Lord, there are hurting and lost people all around me. I ask that You unveil my eyes to see who You are asking me to invest in. I declare I do not have to know everything before I simply approach someone in love. I may not have all the resources or education or even experience that I wish I had to feel more confident, but I know You are faithful. I offer myself to You now. I ask for words of knowledge that I would be able to pray for the one You show me— even if this person is a co-worker or family member. I

*refuse to be ruled by fear. You say I am equipped before
the foundation of the world for such a time as now, so
today is my day to move in communion with Your Holy
Spirit and to pour into the life of the one You show to me.
In the Name and power of Jesus Christ. Amen.*

Give It Away

Who are the orphans and lonely ones around you in need of hope,
healing, and restoration? If the Lord asked you to reach out to one
person today and express His love in a similar way to what you've
witnessed through Ari and June's story, what will you commit to do?
Who can you invite along with you to pray as a Kingdom family?
When will you do it? I'm praying for you! You are born for this. Just
say, "Yes, Jesus."

15

Overcoming

ROCK BOTTOM IS GOOD SOLID GROUND,
AND A DEAD-END STREET IS JUST A
GOOD PLACE TO TURN AROUND.

BUDDY BUIE

The reality of embracing the truth that we belong to God, and even living a lifestyle of surrender to Him, still comes with a set of challenges. It's called being human and living on a less than perfect planet with some steep inclines. Yep, some days I feel like I need an oxygen mask before I have coffee because I made the mistake of picking up my cell phone before I poured my java. Note to self: *Stop doing that. Pray first and listen to the direction of the Holy Spirit. Spend time with Him for a good long while before picking up your cell phone.* This is my reminder.

Most of you are probably more consistent. Most of the time I am disciplined and resilient in choosing to be with Jesus first every morning, but there is the occasion when I lose my mind and pick up my phone first. There will always be more need in the world than we can provide an answer to. The solution the Bible gives us as believers in Christ, functioning in unity as *one* body, is to live our daily lives with a practice of continually asking the Holy Spirit where He has assignments for us. Yes, that will require practice to hear Him in the unique way He speaks to you. The Holy Spirit is more than our Comforter. He functions to glorify the Father and the Son through us. The triune Godhead works in tandem, bringing divine order and glory to God.

In order for the Holy Spirit to glorify the Father and Jesus, we need to actively partner with Him. It is the Holy Spirit who will take away the veil from the eyes of every person, so they will see Jesus. Spending time asking the Holy Spirit about the day ahead and what Scriptures, words of knowledge for healing. or words of wisdom He has is one of the ways He takes the veil from our eyes. We become clouded when we have beheld too much of the world without beholding the glorious King who sits enthroned on high. When we accept the invitation to first fellowship and then partner with the Holy Spirit as a lifestyle, we begin to collectively function as the *unified* Body of Jesus Christ. In this we are doing what Jesus commanded us to do.

If more of us cooperated with Heaven's orders, our pastors and ministers would have far less need for oxygen masks after they open their text messages first thing in the morning. Okay, the Bible doesn't talk about oxygen masks, but I am pointing out the obvious thing. Pastors and ministers are not meant to hold up or heal and deliver all the people. The assignment from Jesus to bring salvation, healing, freedom for the captives and prisoners, and prophesying destiny has always been for *all* believers. When as individuals, pastors or clergy members become the one solely responsible for a flock of people, those people will make that pastor a savior to them. And in turn, pastors will burn out from the undue burden of responsibility placed upon their shoulders.

Jesus raised up apostles, but He did that through deep relationship and life balance. Though the demands upon them were great, Jesus often took His disciples away to secluded places to pray and rest. He empowered them as much through teaching and supernatural impartation as through rest and camaraderie.

Apostles are those who are sent and commissioned to build up the Body of Christ. Jesus sent His disciples and taught them to teach others what they had been taught. This is Kingdom multiplication. Jesus never modeled on ongoing dependency upon one or two people. He told His disciples in John 16:7 it was better that He go away because they would receive power from on high through the Holy Spirit. Jesus set up an ongoing empowerment system created through dependency on the Holy Spirit for all believers.

This is our commission, to bring the full supernatural Gospel to every lost, lonely soul and to introduce them to the fullness of the Holy Spirit and how to develop intimacy with God through His presence. Lastly, we are to encourage them to give away what they have just been given.

If we do not make a change in the standardization of church leadership to include total dependency on the Holy Spirit and a determination to supernaturally empower the entire Body of Christ for the work of the ministry, we will continue to witness pastors, leaders, and social workers coming to an end of their ability to remain buoyant under the weight of human suffering. When we become a Kingdom, a family unified in the mission and vision of Jesus that all will be saved, delivered, and freed, there will be many more of us doing the work of the Holy Spirit en masse. This casts a wide net and establishes a safe place for the newly born again or newly healed ones to find their identity in the Christ community in the love and presence of the Holy Spirit. The good news of Jesus and His signs, wonders, and miracles are to follow all who believe and never specified only ordained clergy.

First Corinthians 12:4-5 in *The Message* reminds us, *"God's various gifts are handed out everywhere; but they all originate in God's Spirit. God's various ministries are carried out everywhere; but they all originate in God's Spirit. God's various expressions of power are in action everywhere; but God himself is behind it all. Each person is given something to do that shows who God is: Everyone gets in on it, everyone benefits. All kinds of things are handed out by the Spirit, and to all kinds of people!"*

But, although we are qualified, we are often afraid and have reasons we don't step up and do what Jesus said we could do. This not only causes the Body of Christ to be actively missing parts and places undo pressure on others, but it eventually creates an atmosphere of hierarchy within the Church. If only the minority of believers actively partner with the Holy Spirit to do the works of the ministry and those individuals happen to be leaders, we end up depending on them instead of moving in unity, empowered as the Kingdom family Jesus established. Many hands make light work.

What is limiting you? I've already covered feeling disqualified in other chapters in regard to helping others in healing and freedom prayer, but here I want to point out the prevalence of eliminating oneself from participation in the works of Christ because of our own human limitation and sin. I admit, being willing to spend your life for Christ to do what God asks launches you into a head-on collision with your own sin and inconsistency. I have often said to the Lord, "Really? You are going to use me? My attitude needs serious adjusting!" Everything we struggle with, take offense to, and cast judgment over we are to bring to the Lord. He is the best attitude adjuster in the universe. Many of us believe we are too far gone and have no grace for the process of being transformed into the image of Jesus. If you are anything like me, you pray God will fix everything about you and then send you out to bring the Gospel. *Just don't send me out like I am, Lord!*

The process of inviting Jesus into our limitations and sin is the process of sanctification covered in grace. Grace is the *unmerited favor* of God and the *empowerment* of His Holy Spirit. Both meanings of *grace* are used many times in Scripture. As you and I embrace God's favor and empowerment for the journey despite our less than desirable attitudes, we will discover through supernatural revelation that God's power and authority is in fact, intact—in each of us. When we embrace His grace, we begin to express grace for others. Grace is necessary for unity in the Body of Christ and unity creates trust.

In Hebrews 4:16 we even find the promise that He gives us mercy and help in our time of need. *Help me, Jesus.* I love that verse. I should order it on a T-shirt and wear it daily to remind myself. I do like changing clothes, so perhaps I need to consider a tattoo on my wrist. Here is Hebrews 4:16 for you, too, in case you want to get a matching tattoo: *"Let us then approach God's throne of grace with confidence, so that we may receive mercy and find grace to help us in our time of need"* (NIV).

Come when you are weary! Come when you are clueless! Come when you are broken and full of doubt and Jesus has mercy and more grace. Wow. Who doesn't need this verse daily?

In moments where I am struggling to overcome an attitude that has wormed its way into my consciousness, I am challenged by the Holy Spirit to stop and take inventory at what has just robbed me of peace. The world can easily cause us to absorb many things contrary to Christ's nature. Since Jesus said that our mind will be kept in perfect peace if we absorb ourselves in Him (see Isa. 26:3), I have obviously absorbed something other than Jesus if I am battling with my frame of mind. Kitchen sink sponges get pretty gross if not thoroughly rinsed.

Come and hose me off, Lord.

The Holy Spirit has hosed me off more than once even in the middle of a church service or healing meeting. I have mentioned how much I love Brazil and being there at any time fills my heart with joy. On a recent occasion, I was there without our Agape Freedom Fighters ministry team, which is an unusual thing for me. I almost always have the team with me because I believe, as I said, that the Body unified and moving together brings incredible change and creates an atmosphere of trust and empowerment for all. This time, however, I was solo. I arrived excited but tired. Long plane rides are physically tiring, but I was weary from ministry busyness over many months. I had not had enough downtime to absorb the Lord's presence afresh, and I missed that communion time. His presence is the bright sunshine of joy that washes away the fatigue—sometimes the tiredness is thicker than San Francisco summer morning fog. On this trip, my fatigue was never constant but would reveal itself through an unwelcome attitude creeping in like an alien invader. This is not normal for me, but I have known times of weariness like this before. Despite the invasion of intermittent fog, the Lord continued in His extravagance and kindness.

Something to take note of here. When we are weak, He is strong, and it is our heavenly Father's good pleasure to not only provide for us but to unleash our full inheritance in Jesus Christ. In Luke 12:32 (NIV) Jesus said, *"Do not be afraid, little flock, for your Father has been pleased to give you the kingdom."* Do not fear ones who belong to Me, you who are My family. Using the term *little flock* makes me smile. When we have little faith, compassion, or wisdom, and when we have little grace for ourselves or others, we still belong to Him and He is shepherding us. In all of our littleness, He is magnificently abundant. The Kingdom is Christ's rule and reign on earth, and all the blessings and advantages belong to us, His royal heirs. All of it available to us even when we are weary and in need of an attitude adjustment.

I had been in Brazil for a week and the extravagant outpourings of the Holy Spirit overwhelmed me in each and every gathering. I was immersed in the faithfulness of God and experiencing again the Father's delight to pour Himself out over the hungry and thirsty. It was now Friday evening, and I began speaking at the evening church service at 10:00 p.m. I love the Brazilian people! Where else in the world do you start worship at 10:00 p.m.? Come on.

After worship, I walked across the expansive platform to preach the Gospel. I spoke of joy as a weapon against the enemy and joy as the fruit of the Holy Spirit according to Romans 14:17. My own heart burned within me at the truth of Scripture. My faith was high, and I began to release words of knowledge for healing over the masses of people gathered. I headed off the platform and down to the people gathered, so I could watch firsthand where the Holy Spirit was moving among His Beloved. The church's well-trained prayer team was interspersed throughout the front of the sanctuary. Many were engaged in praying for specific people as I called them to come up front for ministry from the words of knowledge. The worship team began to worship in glorious adoration to the Lord, and as I was praying from the microphone, two prayer team members approached me and asked me to come with them to pray for a woman.

In an instant, the alien invader swept through my brain. I am very familiar with the enemy and his tactics. He is an opportunist, and because I had been struggling with fatigue and it was now after midnight, he rolled in like a freight train. The assault in my brain was loud.

Why don't the prayer team members take care of that person? Why do I have to go through a crowd of fifteen hundred people and pray for this one? There are all kinds of people who can do it. I was shaken by the assault.

Instead of doing what I have done in the past—to participate in the accusation—I responded from a position of weakness and knew The Lord would respond from a position of strength. In my mind as I turned to follow the two prayer team members I said, "Lord, I am sorry. It is a great privilege to be here and to minister at all. Although I don't understand why I have to go and pray for this person because we have a church full of people who can do it, I will do what You ask."

I felt my hands on fire and heard the Holy Spirit say through a very strong impression, *I know you desire for the Church to rise up and pray, but I am sending you to this woman. Pay attention to what I am doing and look around.* Remember, the enemy has no jurisdiction in our mind, soul, or body unless we give him access.

The enormous sanctuary held close to four thousand people and with COVID restrictions in place, the seats on the main floor were filled with about fifteen hundred lovers of Jesus. As I walked along in front of the platform, I looked into the crowd. What worshipers! The average age for this late-night service appeared to be about twenty-five years of age. This was their service, and they came to glorify God and be touched by the Holy Spirit.

The two women leading me through the crowd continued until we were midway back in the rows of chairs on the left side of the room.

They stopped in front of an older woman with graying black hair and kind brown eyes. She held a cane in one hand, and as I moved in front of her, I watched her eyes well up with tears. The familiar reflection of intense and chronic pain radiated from her eyes. I know that look very well, since I lived with it for such a long time. The worship was loud and in order for me to speak with the woman in need, my interpreter moved next to the woman on her left side between the two of us.

"Hi, I'm Jo! What's your name?" I yelled.

"I am Jacinta, and I watched your video about your healing. Some-one from this church brought me here, so you could pray for me. I am in so much pain." My translator, Nina, yelled the translation into my ear.

I could feel the voice of distraction try to invade my mind again with this thought: *Other people should pray for her. You don't need to be the one. After all, you always say you don't want to be the only one people ask for prayer from.*

I jerked my attention back to the Holy Spirit, and the love Jesus had for the woman in front of me. He had already assured me that He has sent me to this woman, and I was reminded again to pay attention and look around. I paused and looked around the woman. I could not help the smile erupting on my lips. Standing on all sides of this precious woman were the students from the church's supernatural school of ministry I had the privilege of teaching just a few days before. Excitement and faith rose up within me. *Okay, Lord, just tell me what to do.* I followed the impressions I have learned are from the Lord that I saw and heard in my mind. These impressions created eagerness and confidence in what the Lord was about to do.

"Jacinta, if level ten is the worst pain a person can have, what level pain do you have at this moment?"

Before she responded, fresh tears ran down her cheeks. "I have more than ten. Maybe even twelve. I never have time without pain." She cried.

I nodded and looked around. Several of the students caught my eye as they were watching what I was doing. I began asking her about her hip and knee, both without cartilage she reported. I learned through asking a series of questions that Jacinta's condition was a generational degenerative disease manifesting in her grandmother, mother, and aunt. She had been suffering and having progressively worsening symptoms over the past three years. She was unable to move around without debilitating pain.

The Holy Spirit made it very clear to ask her to break an agreement with the words, *I will end up just like my mother. Unable to walk or move without pain.*

As I invited the Holy Spirit to come and take over, I asked the students standing around her to begin interceding for her miracle. I watched their eager faces at being asked to participate. Joy soared through my heart. As Jacinta broke agreement with the words, her hip pain reduced from twelve to three.

"Lord Jesus, I ask that Your holy angels come now and bring brand-new cartilage for Jacinta's hip, and I command all manifestation of this disease and pain to leave in Your name." I felt the increase of the fire of the Lord on my hands as I placed them on her right hip. "Jacinta, tell me what's happening in your hip now."

"I feel heat there, and in my back!" Her face registered shock.

"Will you move around and let me know your pain level now?"

"I have no pain! No pain! Not in my hip but my knee is painful still." She went from exuberance to depression in three seconds. I recognized the enemy trying to steal this healing from her.

"Hey, Jacinta, the Lord is going to heal your knee next, but let's thank Him for healing your hip first, okay?"

"Oh yes, okay, yes!" Along with Jacinta, our interpreter and me, all of the students let out a shout of praise to God.

Okay, Holy Spirit. I see these students all around, and I feel You sent me here for more than just this healing, right?

I could feel God smile.

I put my hand on Jacinta's shoulder and spoke to the interpreter. "These are some of the students from the school and I am going to have them help me pray for your knee, is that okay?"

She nodded.

The interpreter let the students know, and another prompt from the Holy Spirit had me ask the young man called Delmo in the tan suede jacket and jeans standing next to me for help. His smile eradicated all doubt from the area. This was going to be good.

Through the interpreter I explained that Jacinta needed her hips to realign, and as he helped me pray for this, her knee would be healed. Jacinta tried to insist I pray for her knee the same way as I prayed for her hip, but the Holy Spirit was doing something else. I looked into her eyes and asked her to trust Jesus. He would complete what He started. She nodded.

We gently sat her down in a chair, and I asked Delmo to kneel down in front of her and to hold her feet propped on his kneeling knees. Jacinta's legs were stretched out in front of her. As Delmo aligned her heels next to each other, her leg length differed by almost an inch.

I asked many of the students to observe for themselves the difference in length and explained this was due to her spine being rotated and one hip being higher because of the compensation in the way she moved due to the pain in her hip. Wide-eyed students squeezed in closer around Jacinta and whispered to each other. I almost laughed out loud at the perfect Holy Spirit setup. I asked two more students to place their hands on both of Jacinta's hips. Since the cartilage missing was in her left knee, I asked the young woman on her left side to say,

"In the Name of Jesus Christ, I command these hips to align and the hip sockets to have space."

As she spoke the words, the left leg visibly lengthened. Shouts of praise erupted from the students and Delmo's eyes looked as if they would pop from the sockets.

"Delmo, I'd like for you to command Jacinta's spinal column, hips, knees, and ankles to have structural integrity and for brand-new cartilage in her left knee to form now in the Name of Jesus and to declare the end to all dysfunction and pain in her body. Lastly, command the generational spirit of infirmity and his assignment to end now in the authority of Jesus Christ." Once Nina explained what to pray in Portuguese, Delmo went after the healing with courage and boldness. The leg length happening at the Name of Jesus overwhelmed him with faith.

When Delmo finished praying, I said, "Hey, ask Jacinta to stand up and check out her knee, hip, and back."

Delmo radiated enthusiasm from every pore in his body.

As Jacinta rose from the chair, she began shouting, "Gloria a Dios! Gloria a Dios! Jesús es Rey!" (Glory to God! Glory to God! Jesus is King!) She began to jump up and down with fresh tears as the chorus of students screamed the Name of Jesus for all His glory. "I have no more pain. I am healed!"

These precious students had just prayed for their first miracle, and Jesus did not disappoint them or me.

I took Jacinta by the hand and brought her up onto the platform with me.

Almost to the steps of the stage, one of the young men tried to hand Jacinta back her cane.

"She won't ever need that again," I said.

The young man threw down the cane and began clapping as Jacinta took the platform, dancing, jumping, declaring the miracle working power of Jesus and giving all the thanks and glory to God alone. The other students and then the whole sanctuary began cheering for God. Just as it should be. Jacinta overcame by the blood of the Lamb and the word of her testimony. I have a report that even two months after the miracle Jacinta remains pain-free.

I also overcame the troubler of our soul by the blood of the Lamb and Jacinta's testimony. The entire scenario helped me to see once again that despite our shortcomings, failings, weaknesses, and sin, God makes all grace abound to us so that we have more than we need in every situation. Jacinta's miracle undid me but even more spectacular was to see how He placed her in the midst of all of those students and then sent me to heal my own heart in the process.

Despite my fatigue, battling fog and the words of the enemy, the Lord showed up and not only changed a women's life but gave me the opportunity to equip and activate the next generation in a way that classroom learning can't do. When will I learn that Christ made us all more than overcomers?

No matter what we face, the Lord trumps the enemy in every way—when we will just do what He asks.

The desire of my heart is to equip the Body of Christ to do the work entrusted to us by Jesus Christ. I long to release the fullness of the presence of the Holy Spirit, moving in His supernatural power and authority so all people will know the Kingdom has come upon them and God our Father has made a way for all mankind to be free forevermore.

God never asked for perfection from His kids. He only asked for our heart and our willingness. The focus of consistency—being absorbed in God—lies in simply seeking the Lord first and making oneself available. Along the way, we are actually being transformed into the likeness of Jesus. I can complicate anything, how about you?

"Come to me, all of you who are weary and carry heavy burdens, and I will give you rest." That is what Jesus said Matthew 11:28. He also said that our religious works benefit us nothing because according to the book of Romans, we are made holy because of His grace and glory not because of our religious acts. The promise of life in Him is action. When we begin to live convinced in our hearts (mind, will, and emotions) that we already belong to Jesus and have been freely given all access into His supernatural power and authority, then we cannot help but be both compelled and propelled into actions of His great love. Remember, the more we behold our glorious King, Who sits enthroned on high, and the less we behold the shortcomings and obstacles of living in this world, we are limitless! We are not earning something in the action of supernatural ministry but rather fulfilling the destiny of our lives purchased by Jesus.

I live to empower a generation to come to embrace that this destiny is the greatest gift of all. I pray that you do too.

What's Next Activation

Psalm 104:3-4 in *The Passion Translation* describes the Lord and His people in the most glorious way. *"You build your balconies with light beams and ride as King in a chariot you made from clouds. You fly upon the wings of the wind. You make your messengers into winds of the Spirit, and all your ministers become flames of fire."*

Keep this truth in your heart as you pray.

— *Prayer* —

Lord, thank You that You desire to use me even when I am stumbling or uncertain. I have only just begun to discover the riches of Your glorious inheritance in me and through my life. I pray that You show me how to fix my eyes on You alone even when the enemy is trying to have me think thoughts that are not mine. You said if I turn from the enemy, he will flee. Today, I turn back to You and ask that You would prompt me to see with new eyes the ones in front of me who You plan to touch. Help me focus on the one thing—You alone, Lord. Holy Spirit, please give me new courage to invite You to be present with all my conversations either in person or through technology. I am Your minister, and You have made me a flame of fire. Today, I give You permission, Lord. Use me to heal the sick through Your resurrection power. I don't need to go to Brazil to watch You move. You are moving all around me and You've invited me to participate with what You have already planned. Teach me today and heal any division in my heart that would prevent me from moving in union with You.

Give It Away

Sit for a few quiet moments more and ask, *Lord, show me any area where I have not seen You in Your rightful place as Lord over all. Where are the areas of weakness and vulnerability within me that You desire to heal and fortify?*

Write down the impressions the Lord gives to you and ask the Lord to bring healing for the process of your personal transformation. To help you shift your perspective from judgment to grace.

> *Lord, You are fortifying me and sanctifying me. Today, may my actions promote Kingdom unity as I step into the boldness to do what You've asked of me. Help me receive the fullness of Your grace, embracing Your divine empowerment to do what You've asked. To take my rightful place and bring unity to the Body of Christ. Jesus, who and what do You want to heal today? Show me Your plans and details.*

Write down any impressions you have for conditions or diseases, body parts, or emotional struggles you believe the Lord impressed upon you. Now ask Him to remind you of these words and who to release them over as you go about your day. You may end up praying for the person collecting your money in the drive-through window or the person you meet in the hallway in your office. Maybe it is even a family member or friend who calls you unexpectedly. Ask a friend to join you and begin unifying the body. Remember, you and God are a team and you are practicing working with Him. There is no failure—just epic tries.

16

Obstacles Become Opportunity

WHENEVER A CHILD OF GOD EVEN FOR A
MOMENT LOSES HIS PEACE OF MIND, HE
SHOULD BE CONCERNED TO FIND IT AGAIN, NOT
BY SEEKING IT IN THE WORLD OR IN HIS OWN
EXPERIENCE, BUT IN THE LORD ALONE.

CHARLES SPURGEON

God-sized perspective takes yielding, surrendering, and trusting. It takes vulnerability—allowing God to infuse you with hope to believe more in the nature and character of God instead of the circumstances we find ourselves in. Disappointment without Jesus brings bitterness. Disappointment in life through a love relationship with Jesus is a bridge. Cross over and find yourself in the arms of the One who created all things and by divine dominion remains in control of all things—despite confusion or doubt.

Hebrews 11:1 says that *faith is the assurance of things hoped for, and the conviction of things not seen*" (ESV). The love of the Lord is a bridge that allows us to grab on to hope as a means to build faith. Without any hope it is impossible to simply muster up faith. Hope is the catalyst, the spark that builds the flame of faith. Hope is the fertile soil where a tiny seed of faith grows. God's divine love is the living water that nurtures faith and causes it to grow. We cannot circumvent the process. Encountering God's love through ordinary people causes hope to burst forth in the heart of every person. In that moment, the faith seed is planted. It's a supernatural phenomenon, and I never grow weary of watching the creativity of God to cause hope to rise in the most desperate of situations no matter what they are.

There's a huge difference between having faith that God *could* do something or faith that God *will* do something.

In the summer of 2021 I was ministering with our Agape Freedom Fighters team at a house meeting in Southern California. During that meeting I shared this story.

I was ministering at a conference in a New Jersey church. As I finished teaching, the presence of the Lord poured into the building, and I felt the Lord lead me to walk up and down the aisles releasing the words He was impressing on me to speak. In a moment like that, where the Holy Spirit is moving powerfully, prophetic words are designed to encourage hope to release faith. It is what Jesus did when He preached the Word, shared parables, and prayed for the sick. The declaration of the testimony of Jesus—who He is and what He does—is the spirit of prophecy. We always have a choice: We can move with the Holy Spirit or continue with our planned agenda. I have found the Holy Spirit to be so much more enjoyable and creative than my preplanned agenda!

In the tiny church filled to overflowing with expectant people, I stepped off the platform and walked down the left side aisle. I was more than halfway to the back of the church when I had a huge word of knowledge. It felt like flames in my mouth, and I knew I had to say what I was prompted by the Holy Spirit to say. I turned around and pointed to a couple on the front row. I had never met this couple prior to this time, so I would not have known anything about them.

"Would you please stand up?"

A woman in a beautiful multicolored African print dress and a man wearing a light-blue polo shirt and navy-blue slacks stood up.

"In ten months, there will be a baby crying in your house," I declared.

The woman burst into tears, and the man's eyes filled to the brim, about to cascade down his ample cheeks. The power of the Holy Spirit touched both of them deeply and they were eased down into their seats by others before they fell over under the weightiness of the glory.

The Lord continued to move powerfully through the meeting and many were radically healed while others were set free from torment. How I praise God for His extraordinary love!

As the meeting drew to a close, the co-pastor of the church where the meeting was being held approached me. Tifany is a dear friend, and together she and her husband, Mike, pastor locally and are an active part of our Agape Freedom Fighters ministry team. She introduced the beautiful couple to me and asked them to share a bit of their story.

"We have been trying to conceive for eight years," the husband said as his wife broke into fresh tears. "What you spoke over us we have prayed and prayed for, but we have been told by doctors we are medically unable to have children."

I smiled, overwhelmed again by the love of Jesus for these two precious people. "Do you believe the Lord will give you what you desire?"

"Yes!" they said together, nodding.

"Pastor Tifany and I stand with you today in full agreement. Together, we believe the word of the Lord that you will have a baby in your house in ten months no matter what the doctors have said."

Tifany shared her own miracle testimony with them. She and Mike had struggled with infertility for almost eight years, and they, too, received the miracle from the Lord. Their adorable baby girl is now almost three years old. Then we prayed over their reproductive organs and praised the Lord for His faithfulness to do what seemed impossible.

In celebration of the faithfulness of God, we hugged each other goodbye.

A number of months later, I received word from Tifany that this couple was pregnant. Eleven months later I returned to New Jersey, and as this couple handed me their beautiful baby boy dressed in a light-blue terry cloth jumper, I burst into joyful praise for all the Lord had done. I had the privilege of praying for baby Eli at his dedication ceremony. The power of God is unfathomable, and the power of the testimony is a key to unlocking faith.

Now almost two years after the service in New Jersey, I was in the meeting in Southern California on a breezy Friday summer night, sharing the power of God to bring His miraculous creative miracles to pass. The testimony of Eli, even though I had not planned to share it at all, brought the power of the Holy Spirit bursting forth like fire, and throughout the packed house, most were radically touched. The sweet sound of the cello and keys broke out, and spontaneous worship of our Lord poured into the atmosphere. Even those on the sidewalk outside the home stopped to listen and look into the open courtyard. They were openly moved.

Our Agape ministry team moved throughout the crowd blessing people with prayer while a beautiful couple approached me and told me, "We listened to your story of that couple in New Jersey, and that's our story! We have been trying to get pregnant for eight years. Doctors say it's impossible, and we are going to the IVF clinic on Monday. But we believe we won't have to now! I know this testimony is for us!" The woman, Alicen, was a pressure cooker of faith about to blow—it's time! She reminded me of the faith of the woman with the issue of blood. She was not leaving until Jesus touched her.

Her husband, Tony, equaled her faith. "Would you just pray for us?"

"I don't know you people, but I love you!" I laughed. "Your faith is a force. Of course, I will pray. What an honor. I have met thirty-two miracle babies around the world born to barren couples and couples unable to conceive medically, and your baby will be number thirty-three. Let's pray."

As I laid my hands on them, the woman fell under the power of the Holy Spirit and ended up on the floor. Her husband shook under the glorious presence of God.

"Thank You, Lord. Thank You for what You're creating here," I said.

Like a flash of white lightning, the beautiful dog of the house, a white Samoyed named Amelia, came bounding into the living room and kitchen area where many people were laid out under the presence of the Holy Spirit. Amelia charged up and planted a wet, sloppy tongue kiss right into the mouth of the woman on the floor I had just prayed for. A great guffaw erupted from my lips.

My friend Doreen, owner of the dog and the home, ran over. "Amelia, oh my gosh! Stop! What? How did you get out!" Doreen's swift hand motion jerked Amelia by her bright-pink harness and drug her out of the room.

That only propelled my howling laughter. I reached down and grabbed Alicen's hand and helped lift her off the floor.

She burst out laughing. "Wow. That was something." She doubled over, giggling.

Tony joined the joy outbreak and stood holding Alicen's arm. He smiled as large as Texas.

"Hey, well, you just got blessed by Amelia, so that sealed the deal." I hugged them goodbye. "Keep me posted on what happens."

As they walked away still laughing, I heard the Holy Spirit say, *I overshadowed her.*

I marvel at the wildness and wonder of God. This holy moment filled with all manner of distraction and life happenings does not deter God. In fact, I'll be bold and say, I believe the Lord loves real human life. He loves crashing into the middle of it. I am reminded again, Jesus walked on the earth in the fullness of human distraction and life happenings, and He did extraordinary miracles. We are to do the same. Nothing can diminish the power of God.

I flew home on Sunday after two days in Southern California.

My phone lit up with a message from Doreen. *You are not going to believe this Jo! My friend texted me just now! You know—Alicen the one you prayed for that Amelia french-kissed?*

I was laughing all over again in the airport as I continued read the text.

Alicen said she felt on Saturday all day after receiving the word and prayer Friday night that today—Sunday—she should take a pregnancy test. She's pregnant! What? Number 33! They cancelled their IVF appointment! Thank You, Jesus!

I boarded the airplane still smiling and thanking God that He uses simple, ordinary people to release His irrefutable miracle power and presence. Again, and again, there is an invitation. Just spend time with God, learn to hear His voice, do what He asks with humility and love, and live a life that cannot compare to anything else. That is the life, after all that you were destined for from the beginning.

Several months later I received a social media message from Alicen exclaiming her praise to the Lord for her pregnancy and beautiful baby boy growing healthy in her womb. I am overwhelmed with gratitude and cannot wait to meet him. There is nothing God cannot do.

In these couples' lives, testimony and prayer played a huge part in their journey. Hope was released, and faith rose as the love of the Lord through the presence and power of the Holy Spirit overwhelmed each of them.

No matter where you have been waiting for the Lord to move, allow hope to spark within you now.

What's Next Activation

— *Prayer* —

Father, I receive these testimonies and breathe You in. I invite the presence of the Holy Spirit to invade my mind and remove all disappointment and bitterness within me. You are the God of hope. Fill me with the remembrance of the promises of Your Word. Help me, Lord, to find and listen to testimonies of Your miracles instead of meditating on my losses. Take me to gatherings in person or even online so I can join my faith with other hungry believers. You said, when two or more of us are gathered in Your Name, You are in our midst. I believe as I join my small amount of faith with Your Spirit, You are free to move, and I will receive what I am asking You for. Lord, touch me again. I am choosing to walk over the bridge of hope that Jesus is and ask You to cause my faith to grow deep roots. Overshadow me, Jesus. Bring Your perfect healing over _____ (include what is ailing You—mind, body, and soul).

Give It Away

I want to address the potential elephant in the room. I sense the elephant is our struggle with the dual reality we find ourselves in—living in the natural world as fully human and yet seated in heavenly places with Christ (see Eph. 2:6). As believers, we have Jesus' supernatural identity (verses 4-7) and yet live in bodies of flesh. Let me explain. I just shared with you three powerful testimonies of supernatural miracles of God creating babies in their mother's wombs to medically certified barren couples. Even today, you and I both know couples still trying to conceive after years of prayer, fasting, and seeking the Lord in every way. To date, for them, there is no manifestation of a miracle.

The Give It Away question then becomes: What will you do with the crushed and hurting ones who have not received a child even when you or others prayed? What will you do in response to those who, like me, might have been suffering unbearable pain for more than a decade? Maybe that person is you.

I know many in the Body of Christ refuse to continue to pray for things that seem impossible. Still others in the Body of Christ are warned not to release prophetic promises about marriages or children. I understand caution to avoid recklessly hurting people, but if fear prevents us from releasing a word of knowledge to bring forth a miracle for a child or a healing or deliverance, we have missed it. I don't take anything the Lord says lightly—despite how often I burst into laughter. Joy is the mantle I have because the Lord has turned my suffering and mourning of almost fifteen years into dancing! My life and yours is one of ongoing trust. We have a divine privilege to simply spend time with the Lord as our best friend and ask that He birth the miraculous through us, not because we are right but because He is faithful and true.

Today, you may feel God has passed you by. My heart goes out to you as I felt those same feelings many times during my desert years of endless chronic pain. Few would understand the position of being in WAIT better than I do. The acronym W.A.I.T. for me used to mean *waiting anxiously, irritated today*. When I am overwhelmed with the circumstances and disappointment in my WAIT or become frustrated about the perception of a lack of answered prayer for the person I am praying for instead of being overwhelmed by the Lord, I have shifted my focus from supernatural to natural. Because we live in a holy tension on a continuum until we depart from this world, we are called to continuously partner with the power of supernatural truth.

Jesus is the Person of truth Who is seated at the right hand of the Father and He sent us the Counselor, Who is the Spirit of truth. He gave us the Holy Spirit to depend upon. Therefore, we can never let facts be our sole basis for expectation. I realize that sounds ridiculous for the pragmatic among us. But, hear me out. Facts are facts. I don't deny facts. I have instead, adopted an approach I pray will help you. I ask the Holy Spirit what He has to say about the facts instead of assuming the facts dictate the outcome. When I switch to this method of approaching ongoing challenges, I have found wisdom, creative ways of moving forward and yes, even healing and miracles. God has not abandoned you nor forgotten the one you have prayed for one hundred times.

With this in mind, pray again and this time, stop, spend time with God and in humility and thanksgiving, invite the Holy Spirit into your W.A.I.T. Ask Him to invade you with His truth and then turn around and give it away to the next person you pray for—even if that is you. Then your W.A.I.T. will become a Wild, Awesome God Inspires Transformation—both in you and all of those around you.

17

Even Though You Are Tired and Weary

PERSEVERANCE IS THE HARD WORK YOU DO
AFTER YOU GET TIRED OF DOING THE HARD
WORK YOU ALREADY DID.

NEWT GINGRICH

I had been traveling nonstop for many weeks. In the brief moments back home, in between mission trips, I was packing up all of our household goods for our move across the country from California to Tennessee. Note to self: *Clean out the pantry, closets, and the garage every year. Twelve years is a decade too long to accumulate.*

Author and columnist Erma Bombeck, once said, "Once you get a spice in your home, you have it forever. Women never throw out spices. The Egyptians were buried with their spices. I know which one I am taking with me when I go."

As I wearily packed the kitchen pantry, I wondered how I acquired four bottles of turmeric and three bottles of sage. I used sage once on a chicken in 1998. Since shipping three boxes of spices across the country costs a small fortune, I had to purge. With only a few days to pack, I ran around the house like a maniac, cleaning out every nook and cranny. Truth is, the only thing I wanted to purge was fatigue.

Lord, I am so tired. Help.

I instantly felt the presence of the Lord and heard this question in my mind: *Child, who made your schedule and populated your calendar?*

Um. I stopped short as I was walking up the stairs for the twenty-seventh time in fifteen minutes. *Well, Lord, you know very well that I did.* I could sense Him smiling.

What do you think about your schedule right now?

Before I could even think of a response, I felt His love, and I could hear Matthew 11:28-30 almost like a song: *"Come to me, all of you who are weary and carry heavy burdens, and I will give you rest. Take my yoke upon you. Let me teach you, because I am humble and gentle at heart, and you will find rest for your souls. For my yoke is easy to bear, and the burden I give you is light."*

I turned and sat down on the stairs.

Thank You, Father. I really needed this. Teach me a new way of approaching my schedule, but before You do that, will You just help me get the rest of this finished.

I laughed out loud.

Don't get me wrong, I am determined to allow the Lord to teach me to have better margins and rest, but I also needed Him to give me strength in the middle of the mess I made with my overscheduled life. And this is yet another beautiful thing about Jesus. He will take you up on your request to be taught a new way, and then He will meet you right in the middle of the mess you created until you are ready to learn the new way.

My mom used to call me the Energizer Bunny. Maybe some of you remember the marketing campaign of Energizer batteries featuring a large pink rabbit wearing sunglasses and playing a drum. The rabbit would stop quite suddenly with other battery brands because he was out of juice. Once loaded with Energizer batteries, the peppy pink fluff ball would zip around seemingly forever. I am a lot like that bunny minus the large pink suit and the drum. I am reminded lately, though, that the Energizer bunny eventually runs out of power. While my batteries were dead after packing up the majority of our house, I boarded a plane for Europe anyway. I had a mission trip that was planned the year prior.

After a long overnight flight across the Atlantic, Jessika, an Agape team member, and I were being driven ten hours to our destination in Europe. She was as wiped out as I was from her own recent missions trip to Brazil. Five hours into the journey I turned to Jess. "Okay, we are going to have an amazing week. The Lord is going to do crazy and amazing things because we are so exhausted."

Jessika smiled and sunk farther down into the tiny back seat. "Yep, He always does," she remarked. "He is so kind." Then she draped herself over her backpack and fell asleep.

Lord, I need that sleeping anointing. I missed that when You created me.

I prayed and thought about the Lord while Jessika slept. When our attention and affection is focused on the Lord, we will find refreshing even if we are not able to sleep. His holy presence manifests rest to the deepest part of our being.

Jessika and I spent eight days in the mountains with young, hungry, and very passionate lovers of Jesus. The average age at the gathering was about twenty-eight years old. The next generation came great distances from France, Germany, and Switzerland, all longing for more of Jesus while growing through new experiences with the Holy Spirit. As the Word of God was preached and the Holy Spirit invited to come, we witnessed miracles and healings, holy interruptions, and a commissioning for these young ones to bring the supernatural Gospel of Jesus across Europe through the palpable presence of the Spirit of God. If I told you everything the Lord did in that eight-day period, it would take another book, so I will circle back around to the purpose of this chapter.

No matter how tired or weary we are, when we invite God's presence, He will come to do exceedingly and abundantly more than we can hope, imagine, dream, or even think. There is an interesting passage of Scripture the Lord highlighted to me one day that changed my ability to perceive what could be done supernaturally through rest and refreshing in Him.

Genesis 2:8-15 says,

The Lord God planted a garden in Eden in the east, and there he placed the man he had made. The Lord God made all sorts of trees grow up from the ground—trees that were beautiful and that produced delicious fruit. In the middle of the garden he placed the tree of life and the tree of the knowledge of good and evil.

A river flowed from the land of Eden, watering the garden and then dividing into four branches. The first branch, called the Pishon, flowed around the entire land of Havilah, where gold is found. The gold of that land is exceptionally pure; aromatic resin and onyx stone are also found there. The second branch, called the Gihon, flowed around the entire land of Cush. The third branch, called the Tigris, flowed east of the land of Asshur. The fourth branch is called the Euphrates.

The Lord God placed the man in the Garden of Eden to tend and watch over it.

————•◄►•————

Here we get the beautiful picture of Eden and the place where man is to dwell with God. What we see is Eden flowing with water. There is no shortage. Notice the name of the first river—*Pishon.* Pishon in Hebrew means "to leap forth, to spread out and overflowing increase." In verse 11 the Word says that the Pishon or the *overflowing increase* flows through the entire land of Havilah. The meaning of Havilah might surprise you because the text indicates there is pure gold there. Havilah means the following things.

1. To give birth out of pain

2. To writhe or to fall in pain or fear

3. To grieve

4. To be sore pained, sorrowful

5. To tremble

6. To be wounded

7. To twist or whirl in a circular manner

8. A stretch of mud or sandy land

According to one commentary on the meanings of Havilah, each definition seems to represent aspects of our human nature: fear, grief, woundedness, pain, and going around in circles. Genesis 2:11-12 (BSB) says that in the land of Eden named Havilah *"the gold of that land is pure, and bdellium and onyx are found there."* How interesting. The prophetic metaphor God revealed to me here implies that in pain, woundedness, sorrow, and fear is pure gold, aromatic fragrance (bdellium), and precious stones (onyx). Havilah is actually called "the gold laden land," with countless riches. At first glance, a gold-laden land whose name actually means grief and birth out of pain? Stay with me here. The key to everything is the water. There is a river in Eden with four heads. It is one river and also metaphorically represents the river of God. The river is continually flowing without any human intervention.

Remember the last meaning of Havilah I mentioned was a stretch of mud? Man was made of mud (or dirt depending on the translation). In Eden, the living water that flows over the land of Havilah and removes the mud is a wonderful representation of our lives in Christ. Life is in the flow of living water. As the abundant river flowed over the land of Havilah, the gold began to shine through, the sweet fragrances were released, and the precious gemstones were uncovered. Metaphorically, what a picture this gives to us of Jesus as the living water Who restores the human soul. Resting in His presence washes away the mud, revealing all of the riches of His glorious inheritance in us. Remember, the Pishon river means "overflowing increase."

In John 7:38 (TPT) Jesus said, *"Believe in me so that **rivers of living water** will burst out from within you, flowing from your innermost* *being, just like the Scripture says!'"* As we learn to refresh ourselves in His presence, His living water will burst through us and His Kingdom will be spread through the power of the Holy Spirit until all of the riches He deposited into every human being are revealed. Stunning.

With this in mind, I can't resist telling you at least one testimony from our week in Europe because the Lord is amazing, and we can celebrate Him together.

The very last night of the mountain gathering, Jessika and I were out of gas, batteries, and any other manner of energy. We were wiped out. A young dark-haired woman wearing a long, blue, cotton dress approached me. The meeting was officially over for the night, and we had to leave early the next morning for the long car journey back to the airport. Despite what I was feeling, here this young woman stood. I took a deep breath—often my response when I am bone-weary. I remembered praying for her in a prayer line the day before. At that time, she held a restless infant in her arms and shifted her weight side to side. She had cried then and asked me to pray for a list of her serious health ailments. But, because of the large numbers of people in the line and the focus of the Lord to have Jessika and I lay our hands on everyone at that time, I was not able to devote the focused time of healing prayer this woman requested.

"Remember me? You said you would pray for me. I can't leave this place without getting healed. I can't take the pain anymore. My whole body is falling apart. I am the mom of three kids, and I cannot even take care of them." She began to wail.

I looked around to see if anyone else was near to help me pray. Everyone was either lying on the floor receiving from the Holy Spirit or praying for others. This woman was tired and desperate. I was tired and desperate too, but I know the Lord healed me of chronic pain in a moment, and He could do the same for this woman. I'd love to tell you that I had tons of faith at that moment, but that would not be true. I only had tons of fatigue. Jesus said, *Come.* And so that's what I did.

Okay, Lord. I need You. I do not want to pray a prayer model or on autopilot. This woman needs You, and I need You. Holy Spirit, please come and give me Your direction and Your words. I have none of my own.

Then I placed my hands on the frail, sobbing woman. Through the simple action, I felt a connection with the compassion of Jesus for His hurting child standing in front of me. "Will you tell me your name again?" I spoke in a hushed tone less because of fatigue and more because the Holy Spirit seemed to be coming with barely a whisper. I felt like Elijah must have felt at Horeb in First Kings 19:12. I had seen God come like an earthquake and many times like fire, but right now He came in a still small voice. I listened to the Holy Spirit while the woman responded to my question. Multitasking is a spiritual gift.

"My name is Katerina. I have so many things wrong with me. I am so tired. I am exhausted. I don't sleep. I have so much pan." Sobs erupted from her shaking body, and tears streaked her cheeks.

"Katerina, do you believe Jesus can heal you tonight?"

"Yes, but the doctors said that my spine is degenerating, and my abdomen is herniated because of the pregnancies, and I have stomach issues and chronic headaches, neck and back pain. They cut me this way and that way." With a shaking finger, she drew both a horizontal and vertical line in the air. "And I have scars across my whole abdomen. I am in pain all day, every day. The doctors said I will only get worse until I cannot walk anymore! I cannot even breathe."

Hysteria was near. When fear takes over, it is time to step in with love and silence the enemy's voice that robs the person of hope. When you pray for someone, if they recount everything that is wrong with them in great detail, it will steal their hope and rob you of your faith. That is how the enemy loves to move. Figure out a loving way to stop the person from recounting every issue and traumatic thing they have experienced or been told.

"Katerina, look at me, please. Take three very long and deep breaths." I looked into her eyes with love and compassion.

Jesus was there.

When she had finished her third breath, I spoke again. "I am sorry for all of the pain you have endured, but we are not going to focus on what the doctors have diagnosed or speculated. I bless them all and bring you now to the Great Physician, Jesus. He is here now, and He desires to heal you."

"Holy Spirit, we invite you now to come and take over this time of prayer and bring Your holy presence to give Your daughter rest." My hands remained on her shoulders as I continued praying. "Jesus, You are Jehovah Rapha, the divine healer, and You know what Katrina needs."

Within a few seconds, I was reminded what I had heard the Holy Spirit whisper to me earlier. *She has a three-inch diastasis in her abdomen. Start there.* Diastasis means separation. In Katrina's case, her abdominal wall had been pulled apart through multiple pregnancies and exacerbated from multiple surgeries. Instead of the abdominal muscle closing, as is normal after birthing a child, Katrina's abdominal wall remained open with a three-inch gap. The gap created instability in the pelvic floor and spine and caused a myriad of other orthopedic malalignment and dysfunction. I know all of this because this same ailment plagued me after birthing my son. The Lord uses His victory over the pain in our lives to set others free. He is so good.

How incredibly kind of the Holy Spirit to give me a word of knowledge I understood so well. In my exhaustion, I didn't even have the capacity to think. This specific word of knowledge gave me a way forward to pray for Katrina. Because of all of my abdominal surgeries and healing, I could envision the Lord closing her abdominal wall, repositioning her hips and pelvic floor, leveling her pelvic girdle, and aligning her legs to equal length. Lastly, I saw the Lord's hand reposition Katrina's head squarely on the axis of her body.

I began praying for the very first thing I felt the Holy Spirit show me. I placed my hand on her abdomen and commanded the abdominal separation to close in the Name of Jesus. She immediately felt heat and tingling. Each time I prayed for these specific areas, her pain level decreased, her faith increased, and her face displayed a wild excitement as she could physically feel the heat and tingling of the Holy Spirit all over her body. The last thing I had an impression to pray for was for Katrina to break her agreement with fear that she would always be limited and unused by God and for the restorative rest of Jesus even in the middle of raising three toddlers.

When I finished praying for everything I heard and saw in sequence, Katrina did not have even an inkling of physical pain. Glory to God!

"How are you?" I smiled.

"I can't believe it! I can't believe it!" she screamed as she danced around the room. "I don't have any pain. I feel incredible!" Tears of joy flooded her face.

As I watched her twirl like a child, I prayed, *Thank You, Holy Spirit. Thank You, Jesus, for making this so easy for me. You are amazing. Father, Your love is profound. I am so grateful You included me in Your plan to change the world.*

After Europe, Jessika and I flew to Egypt, and there I heard a report that Katrina released her testimony of healing on the last morning of the mountain gathering. As she told all the Lord had done for her, the host ministers did an altar call. They asked any woman who had experienced difficulty or prolonged pain and dysfunction related to childbirth or surgeries to come forward. Twelve women came to the front of the room. As Katrina and the other leaders prayed over these women, all twelve of them were healed. Next, each of them was baptized in the fire of the Holy Spirit just like the disciples in Acts chapter 2.

I knew four of the women who were healed. Each one has a life that is full to bursting. Lives without margin or rest. What each of these women needed was healing, but what they and what we need beyond healing is a lifestyle that prioritizes the presence of God through rest and balance.

What's Next Activation

What is your usual response when you're tired and weary? How has the Lord shown up for you in the past when you have invited Him into the weariness? What will you take from this chapter that will help you next time you experience dry bones and a weary heart?

— *Prayer* —

Put on instrumental soaking music and find a comfortable place to sit or lie down. Breathe in deeply. Don't rush.

> *Here I am again, Lord. Tired and weary. I am not sure how to approach You in my fatigue, so I will just come as I am, because that is what You say for us to do. I am heavily burdened, and I need rest, but I know even when I am fatigued, You can still use me. Help me break the lie that I am not useful to You when I take breaks or slow down. Show me a new way this week of balancing my life and output while inviting You in. Holy Spirit come and show me the living water that flows inside of*

me. This living water is You, Lord. Jesus, You are my life force. Reveal to me what this living water within me is designed to produce. As I rest and breathe You in, inspire me with Your love, and flood me with Your overwhelming presence.

Give It Away

Paul must have been one of the weariest sojourners the Lord has ever had. Hard-pressed on every side, he wrote often about his weakness and boasted only in the strength of God (see 2 Cor. 4:8-14). I am certain that without the continual presence of the Holy Spirit, Paul would have given up. For those of you, like me, driven in life to achieve goals, it can be even more challenging to comprehend. But, I have learned these past eight years of doing missions for the Lord that He actually delights when I don't know what I am doing or when I run out of myself. With no ideas or energy to move forward, the Lord shows up!

Let me share this lest you become a burned-out missionary. If it is time to rest, please rest. On the other hand, if the Lord is inviting you to experience Him moving through you despite your weariness, take Him up on the invitation. How do you know when to rest and when to engage? Ask the Lord. When I am tired, I ask the Lord if there is anything I need to be doing.

I often hear this: *There are many things, dear child, that you believe you have to do, but I want you to come away with Me now. I will show you a better way, and you will still get everything done.* He is so kind.

Ask the Lord about your to-do lists and projects. Inquire about the people you feel responsible for. He will lead you into His loving embrace and tell you when to rise and when to rest.

As you learn to engage with the presence of the Holy Spirit to bring balance to your life, invite someone else to experience this time of refreshing with you. We have so many weary ones in need of rest.

18

Opportunity Knocks

OPPORTUNITIES ARE LIKE SUNRISES.
IF YOU WAIT TOO LONG YOU MISS THEM.

WILLIAM ARTHUR WARD

I love the quote above by William Ward, but the truth is, the sun will rise again tomorrow, and the invitation and opportunity to partner with God in doing the supernatural works of Jesus will come again. That being said, the unfortunate thing with our decision to avoid seizing an opportunity that God presents is this: The specific moment that God desired to release His presence through our cooperation is lost. Please don't fall into condemnation here. We have all missed many moments. I want to express and incite hope not guilt.

When we agree to step forward, there is a blessing that God gives *to* us as well as *through* us. One of the gifts through obedience is increased boldness. When we witness God moving through our ordinary lives, we are much more excited to partner with Him next time. Another priceless gift we receive is an increasing level of discernment for what the Lord desires to do. We receive what I like to call the "Holy Spirit radar." This radar is prophetic insight. It is developed through practice. People in the world call it perception, while I know it is prophecy. It is learning to hear our best Friend's voice. Over time, each of us, in our own unique way, will have the ability to detect the subtle clues the Lord gives to us through our supernatural unity.

Second Peter 1:3-4 (TPT) says it all:

———— • ◆ • ————

Everything we could ever need for life and godliness has already been deposited in us by his divine power. For all this was lavished upon us through the rich experience of knowing him who has called us by name and invited us to come to him through a glorious manifestation of his goodness. As a result of this, he has given you magnificent promises that are beyond all price, so that through the power of these tremendous promises we can experience partnership with the

*divine nature, by which you have escaped the corrupt desires
that are of the world.*

We have been given all that we need through the supernatural power of Jesus. He has divine opportunities throughout our everyday life. The more intimately connected we are to Jesus, the more aware we are that His promises to include us in His supernatural partnership have already been established. These holy assignments come with God's full approval: An approval from Father to child. An approval fully given without being earned.

Throughout the day-to-day, God's divine invitations are extended to us with great grace to accomplish the fullness of what He established before you and I were even born. How wild. Our continued, singular "yes" to Jesus lessens our interest in the things of this world that vie for our attention and keep us focused on what our natural eyes cannot see.

A few weeks ago, in the early morning, I was worshiping God, and I prayed this simple prayer:

> *Lord, I have been packing up my house for the move and
> have been distracted almost every day. I know I've been
> going on the mission's trips where You send me, but I
> haven't paid attention to what You might be doing with
> anyone in front of me as I am living my everyday life.
> I've only been focused on tasks or praying for others in*

a scheduled prayer meeting. I know Your heart to touch people everywhere, Lord, and I have missed You in these moments. I'm sorry.

I didn't have any compulsion from guilt but rather a hunger to watch God overwhelm one of His beloved children as I went about my everyday life. Though I was on a mission's trip at the moment, I wasn't in a ministry meeting or conference. I was in a hotel fitness center, walking on the treadmill. I felt a nudge from the Holy Spirit to look up. Through the glass windows I saw the enclosed hotel swimming pool, and on the right side of the pool a housekeeper was mopping the floor. As I watched her move, I noticed a pronounced limp. She was favoring her right leg. *Lord, what would you like me to do?* I prayed.

My child, you brought up the subject of doing things with Me again in your everyday life.

Now I could feel the Lord's good pleasure.

Joanne, if you would like to pray for this precious daughter, I am with you.

I love the Lord. Jessika was on the treadmill next to me.

"Hey, Jess, that housekeeper in the pool area is limping. I think she has back pain. Do you want to go and pray with me?"

"Come on! Yep. Let's go." Jess jumped off the treadmill, and we entered the pool area.

As we walked more closely to the housekeeper, I noticed another housekeeper emptying the towel bin on the other side of the pool. Jess and I smiled as they looked at us approaching the uniformed housekeeping with the limp.

"Hello. Excuse me for interrupting. But do you have back pain?"

The woman stared at me and held up the hand that wasn't holding the mop. "No hablo inglés," she said in a heavily accented voice. Jessika speaks some Portuguese, so we limped along trying to communicate but to no avail. The other housekeeper stopped working and watched us from a distance.

"Jo, let's just use Google Translate," Jess said. Then she typed in, *Do you have back pain?* We showed the woman the screen.

"No tengo dolor de espalda," she replied. Again, using Google Translate we understood that she had no back pain, but before I could even inquire of the Lord why I thought He had given me a word of knowledge about back pain, she pointed to her right foot. "Me duele el pie."

Jess said, "Oh, she has pain in her foot!"

I no longer cared that I missed the word of knowledge. This woman was engaging with us by volunteering where her pain was. We knew that God desired for us to partner with Him, so she could experience His presence. "Jess, will you type in, 'Can we pray for you? We believe Jesus wants to heal your foot.'"

Podemos orar por tí. Creemos que Jesús quiere curarte appeared on Jessika's phone screen.

"Sí." The woman flashed a smile, set down her mop, and proceeded to sit down on one of the pool loungers. We nodded as she took her shoe and sock off. Jess and I knelt down to be at the same level as her eyes. When she removed her sock, we both saw a surgical scar almost a half of an inch wide that nearly circled her entire ankle.

I felt the Lord's joy at this divine setup. Neither party spoke the other's language, and here was the Holy Spirit doing what He does best—transforming lives in the middle of an ordinary day.

We asked her what her pain level was through Google Translate, and she replied a level 8 out of 10 with 10 being the worst pain. My heart flooded with the compassion of the Lord for this woman working so hard and having to endure this level of pain. I smiled at her while Jess and I laid our hands on her foot.

We invited the Holy Spirit to come and begin by praying for all of the trauma to be removed from every cell in the tissue of her foot and ankle. We didn't know for sure if she had been in a severe accident or had undergone extensive surgery. We had impressions of these things. We were not dependent on information; we were engaged with the Lord, Who had a burning desire to heal His daughter.

After we prayed for trauma to be removed, she reported her pain level at a level 6. The next two times we prayed for the supernatural re-creation of all the broken bones and severed tendons and ligaments. By the end of the third prayer, all of her pain was gone and she was able to get up and walk without a limp.

"¡Gracias, no tengo mas dolor!" (Thank you, I have no pain!) she said to Jess and me.

"Oh, don't thank us. It's all about Jesus. He healed you."

Although she didn't understand what I said, she beamed at the Name of Jesus. "¡Oh, sí, Jesús! Yo conozco a Jesús." (Oh yes, Jesus! I know Jesus.) She kept repeating, "Thank You, Jesus," as she got up to retrieve her mop as the other housekeeper smiled and clapped. She witnessed the entire thing.

Yes and amen. Jess and I made a heart sign with our hands and pointed up toward heaven.

This time both housekeepers nodded.

Jesus is the only Name that transcends language and cultural barriers. He is our divine Partner for the supernatural life, and there is no greater name or any other life that can compare to one done with Him.

Jess and I walked out of the pool enclosure smiling.

"That was cool," she said. "Too bad she didn't speak Portuguese. It would have been way easier."

I laughed as we returned to the gym to finish working out.

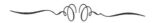

You and I will have countless invitations from our gracious heavenly Father. Remember, the sun rises again. If you miss the moment of opportunity, there is a specific element of grace and provision that is there for the moment. But the Lord is kind, and He will offer you another moment.

But let me make one distinction. In an earlier chapter I mentioned my friend Blaine Cook teaching me that joining God in what He is already doing is much easier than going about praying for someone because they have a need. I am not saying we don't pray for someone in front of us who has a need. I want to clarify: There are strategic moments throughout the day where is God prompting you to supernaturally focus in a given moment. When you learn to sense the nudges and act upon the subtle impressions He gives, there is a profound ease in moving in unity with the Holy Spirit. That is what I mean when I say there is a specific element of grace and provision on the invitation from God and our immediate response to move out and partner with Him.

I could have ignored the nudge to look up as I walked on the treadmill, and I would have missed the miracle of the housekeeper's healing. No condemnation here; I want to encourage you. By jumping off the treadmill at that exact moment, Jessika and I were able to step into a preplanned divine encounter and the Lord brought His fullness despite our stumbling with language barriers.

As we focus on the opportunities that the Lord extends to us, I want to make sure to include the important role that peace plays in all of this.

People with a singular focus on God live much of their life in supernatural peace. Peace is the manifestation of a life in Christ because we learn to trust God. Isaiah 26:3 (ESV) says, *"You keep him in perfect peace whose mind is stayed on you, because he trusts in you."*

It is pretty challenging to step into God opportunities without supernatural peace. Okay, let me make clear that it is normal to have nervousness and uncertainty when you approach someone to pray for them or prophesy a word of encouragement. But if you trust God, the peace will come as you practice. I am speaking about the ongoing supernatural development of a life of peace that comes from living in assurance that you are loved, equipped, and empowered by the Holy Spirit.

Will God show up when you pray or step out in faith?

I can assure you that He desires to show up when any of His beloved ones pray.

Hebrews 11:6 (NIV) tells us that *"without faith it is impossible to please God,"* but there is a connection between faith and trust. It is impossible to have faith if we don't trust God to show up when we pray.

When I experience upheaval in my personal life, I sometimes struggle believing that God will come and move when I call upon Him. This reaction happens because my personal struggles and distractions have reduced my perspective of God's response to me. Instead of focusing on His divine majesty, I am consumed with worldly trials and inwardly trying to calculate how unholy I have been because of what is happening in my life.

The truth is, maybe in a certain season you and I haven't been able to get up super early to spend as much time with God as we normally do, or perhaps we didn't seize the last five opportunities that He gave to us to do supernatural things. As a result, we experience guilt and condemnation. If this happens, rise up, dust off, and don't allow this to mindset to take root again. We already addressed performance orientation earlier in the book. Any shred of this old man or old lady (our fleshly nature) needs to be put to death the instant it rears its ugly head. Use the Word of God as the sword it is designed to be. You and I are the righteousness of Christ. Pray Romans 3:22-24 and watch that old lie of performance fall away. In *The Passion Translation* Romans 3:22-24 says, *"It is God's righteousness made visible through the faithfulness of Jesus Christ. And now all who believe in him receive that gift. For there is really no difference between us, for we all have sinned and are in need of the glory of God. Yet through his powerful declaration of acquittal, God freely gives away his righteousness. His gift of love and favor now cascades over us, all because Jesus, the Anointed One, has liberated us from the guilt, punishment, and power of sin!"*

I pray it penetrates your heart. The righteousness of God is visible in and through your life because you believe in Jesus. That's it. Refocus your mind and your affection on Jesus and find yourself in perfect peace. The peace that is possible as we embrace the fullness of all He is. When you run out of new things to discover about Jesus, read the Gospels again and again. Ask the Holy Spirit to reveal new things through the Word and celebrate that Jesus is more than your wildest dream! I feel like bursting into song as I type this, and maybe you do too. Go ahead, sing like only Jesus is listening and add some dance moves too. Jesus is a superior dancer.

In 2013, after I was healed I was learning to say yes to the Lord. When I worried, I felt the Holy Spirit invite me to sing and more often to dance. These simple acts reduced me to a child more than once and allowed me to receive the words of John 16:33: *"I have said these things to you, that in me you may have peace. In the world you will have tribulation. But take heart; I have overcome the world"* (ESV). The position of Jesus is victorious over whatever the world throws at you. His dominion as ruling King remains no matter what you are experiencing. His affection for you as an approving Father never changes because He overcame the world just for you...and He really loves a good dance partner.

What else hinders our ability to offer a "yes" to God in any given moment? Here's one: The enemy loves to keep us all busy and distracted so we hesitate in joining the Lord in releasing the Kingdom.

I have heard the Holy Spirit say, *The peace I have given to you will never end but neither will the demands of the world upon your time. When demands move ahead of My peace, you will have less stable footing and be prone to missing the step I have set before you. The road is rugged, but in the secret place with Me you will find level ground and sure footing.*

I have been hiking in some crazy places, and the unlevel ground is challenging. When you add ground instability into the mix, it's easy to fall off the cliff. I'd much rather walk in level places, and that will only come for me and for you when we come back to the Lord no matter how often we are distracted, overrun, or hard-pressed. I know the Lord is compassionate and desires that none perish, so He will ask others to come along with Him until one of His children says yes. I pray that we will want to be His "yes" people all the time. It is what we are built for.

I want to talk about a group I have found will say yes to just about anything God is doing: children. As soon as you introduce a child to the Holy Spirit and Jesus' interest in partnering with them to heal and love people, kids are in! My friend has a three-year-old who had witnessed her seven- and nine-year-old brothers fall out under the power of the Holy Spirit. She came over to me and held her hands out in front, saying, "Do me next!" seven times this little blonde cutie fell out under the glory of God, and she still wanted more. Her parents eventually scooped her up amid shrieks of laughter and joy. Children are sponges, and when you show them that God is the most powerful superhero, their lives are impacted forever.

I was doing a ministry meeting on the East Coast. There were many doctors, nurses, and other medical professionals in the healing equipping and training meeting. Some of them were curious about supernatural healing while others came for their own healing. Not everyone believed in Jesus. There were pockets of faith in the room, but doubt and fear were also palpable. The Lord moved powerfully on the worship team before the meeting had even started so we were greatly encouraged of His desire to do amazing things. While we prayed for the worship team, I noticed the only two children in the room belonged to one of the worship leaders. It was a casual observation but one that would prove to change the entire trajectory of the evening.

With worship winding down with a quieter meditation instrumental, I walked up to preach. I looked around the large church hall as I am prone to do, so as to engage with everyone. I desire that every single person understands—when they attend any meeting with the presence of the Holy Spirit, it is because of the Lord's divine invitation. When they said yes to being there, it was the Lord who drew them in.

The evening was sweet with God's presence, and when I asked our Agape ministry team to come forward to release prophetic words and words of knowledge, the Lord began to break out with radical healings. We moved from sweet to fire as the Holy Spirit swept into the room and healed those long suffering with back injuries, residual effects of a stroke, migraine headaches, stomach issues, and more. I asked those who had been healed to stand with our prayer team and pray for those suffering with the same condition they had just been healed from. That is how the Kingdom works: When you receive healing and turn around to pray for another, your faith for that person to be healed is catalytic. A huge percentage of the time, the person receiving prayer from one who has just been healed yields miracles. Faith moves mountains.

We continued praying for people and releasing testimonies of those who had just been healed when a petite woman of about forty years of age, wearing a black knee brace on her right knee, came up to the front. "I had someone pray for me over there and my back is a little bit better, but the pain is still there," she said. "I was in a car accident, and I have no cartilage in my right knee. I am in chronic pain both in my back and my knee." She introduced herself as Debbie.

"Debbie, hang on right here by me and let me have our team pray for you again."

I called our ministry team over, and in five minutes Debbie reported the pain remained.

Holy Spirit, You are obviously working in this room. I want to honor what You are doing, so what do You want me to do? I had an immediate impression of the two little children ages four and seven that I had seen earlier with the worship leader earlier in the evening. I smiled. *Yes and amen, Jesus. Thank You.*

With the microphone in hand, I pointed to the two children sitting in the third row next to their mom. I looked their mom and said, "Would you mind if I borrowed your kids for a little while?"

She smiled and nodded her head.

"Hey, kids, come on up here!"

They ran forward as if they were about to enter the Disneyland gates.

This is better than Disneyland, Lord, and they are about to find that out.

"What are your names?"

They looked wide-eyed at their mom for her approval.

Again, she nodded and smiled.

"I'm Josiah, and I'm four," said the dark-haired boy wearing a yellow T-shirt and faded blue tennis shoes. He had one white sock falling down around his ankles.

"Hi, Josiah! I'm Jo."

He put his hands behind his back and swayed side to side in anticipation of what we were about to do. He didn't look like a boy who enjoyed having to wait very long, so I made my introductions to his sister brief.

"What's your name, sweetie?" I asked her.

She was dressed in pink from head to toe. As she lifted her head to look into my face, her long pink hair bows fell down around her ears. "I'm Rose," she said barely above a whisper.

"Hi, Rose, I'm Jo. And I'm so glad you guys are here. You are so important to Jesus, and He loves you so much."

They both smiled at me and promptly looked over their shoulders and back at their mom once more. She was beaming.

"Josiah and Rose, this is Miss Debbie," I said over the microphone.

Our Agape ministry team took a step back away from Debbie and grinned.

"Miss Debbie has a hurt back and a hurt knee, and I hoped you two would pray for her with me. Is that okay with you guys?" I put the microphone in front of their mouths

"We never prayed for nobody," Josiah said a little too loudly.

I suppressed a giggle. "That's fine, Josiah. I'll teach you. Rose, is this good for you?"

She stood a little straighter. "Um, I think so if you tell us what to say."

Lord, what do you want them to focus on first? Her knee or her back? Working with another impression, I felt that Debbie had been receiving prayer for her back and the pain remained, but nobody had, yet, prayed for her knee. I decided to have the kids pray for the knee first because the impression came so quickly. "The great thing about Jesus, you two, is that He already wants to make sure Miss Debbie isn't in pain anymore, so we are going to pray something quick and simple. Will both of you put one of your hands onto Miss Debbie's knee? It's the one with the black bandage on it."

In less than a second two hands were on Debbie's knee.

Debbie looked incredulous that these two little ones were going to pray for her. She was amused but didn't appear to have great faith. I knew it wouldn't matter what level of faith she had—Josiah and Rose were God's instruments of healing.

"Okay, guys, now, pray this prayer after me: 'Pain, get out in the Name of Jesus.'"

Together in unison, Josiah and Rose repeated, "Pain, get out in the Name of Jesus."

"Now ask Miss Debbie to test out her knee and try something she couldn't do before."

Before the kids could get the words out, Debbie began bending her knee. "What! That is impossible! I had level 10 pain a second ago, and now it's all gone!"

As Debbie squatted up and down doing things she had not done in more than two years, Josiah and Rose jumped up and down bursting with joy. "Let's do it again!" yelled Josiah.

"Miss Debbie, the kids would like to pray for your back. Is that okay?"

"Okay? Come over here, kids! Yes! Yes! Yes!" she yelled.

Josiah's other sock slid down around his ankles as jumped up and down.

"Josiah and Rose, are you ready?"

"Yes!" they shouted more than once.

"Put your hands onto Miss Debbie's back, but first ask her where the pain is. Once you know where her pain is, put one hand each on the spot just like you did with her knee. Jesus just healed her knee when you prayed, so I believe He will heal her back too. How about you?"

"We believe it!" they said as they laid their hands onto Debbie's lower back. I did not have to tell them twice what to pray. Josiah launched in first. "Pain get out, in the Name of Jesus and go back to hell where you came from."

I almost fell in half laughing. I looked over at his mother.

Her face could tell a thousand stories. Instead she mouthed, *I did not teach him that!*

Our whole team dissolved into laughter.

Debbie was immediately healed with Josiah's simple prayer, even with his added dramatic flair. She laughed and cried simultaneously over her miracle while she danced around with both kids. "Thank You for these children, Jesus. Thank You!" she repeated many times.

Despite our team moving next to a time of releasing prophetic words over the crowd, Josiah and Rose continued to run around the room praying healing for anyone and everyone who willingly identified themselves as a candidate. I heard, "Go back to hell where you came from," more than twenty times. I laughed out loud each time I heard it. Every single person Josiah and Rose prayed for in the meeting was healed by the power and blood of Jesus. Some were nurses and one was a doctor. Josiah and Rose didn't care who anyone was or what they did for a living. They simply prayed in the Name of Jesus in the exuberance of a child at play. God is their superhero, and I pray they never outgrow this level of supernatural faith.

Because of their level of faith and freedom, we saw an increase in the number of miracles that night. They were God's secret breakthrough weapon. You are His secret weapon, too. Come in childlike wonder and pray—even when you don't know how. Trust Him and breathe in peace. Watch what Jesus will do.

What's Next Activation

What would you have to believe in order to adopt childlike faith? What are you willing to do about it? Journal what the Holy Spirit impresses upon you. Now, ask the Holy Spirit for the areas of your life to grow in trusting Him so you will be kept in perfect peace. Since we become what we behold, we must behold Jesus as Lord and Lover in every single part of our lives. As we behold Him, peace becomes our countenance.

When you invite a small child to do the things Jesus did, they will clamor and beg to do more. Once you reveal the presence of the Holy Spirit to them and through them, they will believe that God can do anything. I am convinced if all of us had been encouraged and trained up in the supernatural gifts of the Holy Spirit, we would not have such a difficult time today.

Prayer

Although I have written in an earlier chapter about empowering the younger generations, our focus here speaks specifically to teaching children to pray for the sick. My friends Julie and Troy have five kids, and since the time that they were all infants, they have been taught by their parents to pray for everyone. Even as young as six months old, they would eagerly stretch their hands out to place them on someone their siblings were already praying for. They know they are world changers because Jesus told them they are.

Do you have little children you can teach to help you to pray? Ask the Lord in prayer where you can empower children around you. Write down all the ideas and scenarios you are impressed with. Now ask the Lord which one to start with and begin. Grab a friend to join you. Two together is even more fun.

Give It Away

If you have no children to invest in around you, look around at the children who might be near you as you pray for someone. From supermarkets to gas stations, there are children waiting to discover that the Kingdom of Heaven happens through them, no matter how small. When you find a fellow believer desiring prayer, ask if you can invite their children to pray for them. Watch what the Lord will do. It will increase your faith to believe for breakthrough in anything when you watch little ones pray.

19

Open My Eyes

DEATH IS NO MORE A PASSING FROM ONE ROOM
INTO ANOTHER BUT THERE'S A DIFFERENCE FOR
ME, YOU KNOW. BECAUSE IN THAT OTHER ROOM
I SHALL BE ABLE TO SEE.

HELEN KELLER

As I reflect on this favorite quote of Helen Keller, I often think of what my Christian life was like before I fell in love with the Holy Spirit. I was blind. It wouldn't be news to you if you have been walking with Jesus even for a short time, that without spiritual rebirth our sight is veiled, and we have no access to the knowledge of the supernatural life we are born for. The Holy Spirit is the ongoing revelation of Jesus Christ and if we desire to be transformed into the image of the invisible God as the Bible tells us we will be, a continual revelation of Jesus is the ultimate journey to discovering the purpose of our existence. There are moments that mark us forever in our relationship with God and having our spiritual eyes opened oftentimes comes over a period of time. We have blind spots concerning God and His Kingdom until we give the Holy Spirit complete access to our hearts. I am fairly simple with my analogies, so here is one that has helped me illustrate my point.

My husband, Mike, and I fell in love, and over the last twenty-three years we have become the greatest of friends. I know my husband well. I can finish his sentences; I know what he likes and dislikes. I sit with him most mornings when I am home from mission travel and have coffee with him first thing. Here we share conversation or sometimes rich silence. We simply enjoy each other's company. If at any given point in our relationship I get up from the couch and just talk about how great my husband is instead of spending intimate time with him, my perspective of who Mike is becomes based on the revelation I have about him in the past. Like me, Mike is being transformed by the Lord from glory to glory and strength to strength. If I remain close to him, I am aware of the new things about him. My blind spots are uncovered through intimacy, and I see Mike for who he is in greater ways as the years go by.

We are in a relationship with the Holy Spirit. He opens our eyes to see things unlike anything we could ever imagine is possible. If you have been a believer for any length of time, you already know that no one can come to the Father except through Jesus, and it is the Father drawing us near. When I first felt the irresistible tug on my heart by God, I had my eyes opened to the sin that had entangled me. Being aware of my own sin propelled me into the arms of Jesus, and when I gave over my heart and all control to Him, I began to have the truth of the Kingdom revealed to me through the Word of God. The Holy Spirit has given me spiritual eyes to see. He is my Counselor, Teacher, Partner, and the One who daily opens my spiritual eyes to the things most important to our Lord. Time with Jesus comes through the Holy Spirit. No matter what is happening to you or through you, the Lord desires that His fullness in each of us is realized and that comes only through increasing revelation of God. Because the Lord is uncontainable and His Spirit without boundaries, there is no limit to what He can and will do through ordinary people who will willingly spend intimate time with Him instead of walking around just saying great things about Him.

The Kingdom of God is a paradox. We are called to receive ongoing revelation from the Holy Spirit and for most of us, we might assume ongoing revelation comes from great study. Let me state emphatically one more time, I love the study of the Word of God, and I fully know it is necessary for our maturity and understanding. Okay, whew, now that I have clarified the tripping hazard let me jump back to my point. In Matthew chapter 18 Jesus says that revelation about the Kingdom comes in a unique way. In verse 3 Jesus instructs us to come to Him *"like little children."* Children are full of curiosity as much as they are full of need. Curiosity is not uncomfortable for most of us, but being in great need is another thing entirely. Sometimes, the more knowledge we believe we have about God and how He works leads us to a place of no longer recognizing our desperate need for Him.

Paul wrote in First Corinthians 8:1 (NIV), *"Knowledge puffs up while love builds up."* This section of Scripture concerns the disunity happening in the early church about eating food sacrificed to idols.

Check out verses 1-3 in *The Message*: *"The question keeps coming up regarding meat that has been offered up to an idol: Should you attend meals where such meat is served, or not? We sometimes tend to think we know all we need to know to answer these kinds of questions—but sometimes our humble hearts can help us more than our proud minds. We never really know enough until we recognize that God alone knows it all."*

Children assume their parents know everything. They are not concerned with rituals and rules until they are taught restriction. I remember arguing with my friends about who had the smarter father when I was a child. It makes me laugh now. As an adult, I know my father very well and I know his fallibility almost as well as I know my own limitations and sin. But I witnessed the transformation in my father that only Jesus can bring. My father struggled to know the Lord all his life—he was a smart man, educated, and successful. Much of his struggle to know the Lord or to even fathom God's existence I attribute to the belief he held that he already knew everything. He never quite found a way to have a relationship with God because the academic approach to knowing God yielded little satisfaction. Yet as I traveled the world, I shared the testimonies of Jesus' miracles, signs, and wonders with my father, and curiosity erupted from him like champagne bursting out of a newly uncorked bottle. I prayed for his health, and he was healed many times. Through the power of shared testimony and his personal experience of supernatural healing, I saw the child within my father emerge.

He surrendered his life to Christ at 81 years of age, and the revelation of Jesus Christ was revealed to a man who had made a practice of experiencing life through knowledge alone. Before his death a few years later, he would call me. "Squidly"—I know, I'm too old to be called by my childhood name but what can you do?—"tell me where you've been and what God has been doing."

I would share a crazy miracle, and my dad would laugh and cry often within the same moment. Curiosity invited revelation. My dad was being built up in love, and the knowledge that puffed him up for years no longer mattered.

Coming to Jesus in childlike wonder is the only way to discover and enter the Kingdom. Along our journey as we keep the intimate relationship with Jesus first, we study and apply the Word of God in tandem. The supernatural revelation knowledge that comes through intimacy with God influences our study of His Word. There is an overflow that is created through our parent-child relationship with God the Father. His love and acceptance of us causes us to actually believe we can do what He says is possible. When you get intimidated, tell yourself this, "My Dad is the smartest Dad in the whole universe and I can do anything because He says I can." Now that is childlike faith! When you pray for people with this level of simplicity the one in front of you will experience the Kingdom of Heaven on earth. That is just the way God planned it. This process of curiosity, revelation and dependence brings complete transformation.

I met a little girl recently whose own transformation reminded me again that the Gospel is simple and the power and authority of Jesus Christ, is beyond measure.

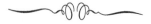

For three days the skies opened up, and rain poured down on a 15-acre parcel of land in the middle of Kentucky. The shallow rivers gathered depth and momentum in the middle of the field, and a large swamp began to emerge. Even with gravel spread over a large section, I watched as the tires of RVs and cars entering the property were held like cement by the deep brown mud. Dozens of strangers standing in the rain came to push or help tow the vehicles so that more could enter the revival. There is a hunger growing in America, and it was a privilege to be part of a tent revival where more than a thousand people gathered for almost a week to both minister to the Lord and be encountered by Him. As the Gospel was preached each night, hundreds of people standing in thick brown mud had their blind eyes opened to the love and freedom in Jesus Christ. Hallelujah. Horse troughs doubled as baptismal pools and ankle-deep mud sucked the pools even deeper into the ground. Despite the rain and mud around them and in the pools, the lines of people waiting to be baptized grew each night. I was undone by the salvations, healings, and miracles I was witnessing, but the moment I saw Jesus and the power of the Holy Spirit encounter a tiny seven-year-old girl, I was undone.

"Jo, there is a lady at the bottom of the steps," a young leader whispered in my ear, as I stood on the platform ready to pray with other pastors and leaders. "And she says she knows you from Global Supernatural School of Ministry and she needs to speak to you about what happened to her daughter."

"What does she want to tell me?"

The woman speaking to me looked into my eyes. "I don't know, but the little girl is really experiencing the Holy Spirit."

I headed for the metal stairs and saw a woman I had met while teaching the month before at Dr. Randy Clark's supernatural school of ministry in Pennsylvania. In front of her stood a beautiful, soaking wet brown-haired petite little girl. She was shaking, gripping a multicolored towel around her body. Tears ran down her face and mixed with the drips coming from her saturated hair. Her mom was crying too.

"Hi," I said to the mom. "Are you guys okay?"

"My daughter, Claudia, has to tell you what happened. She has never wanted to come up front and talk to anyone, but she says she has to tell you. She said she needs to tell everyone here!"

The presence of the Holy Spirit was palpable, and the hair on my arms was standing up. I knelt down in front of Claudia, so I could look into her beautiful brown eyes. "Hi, sweetie, do you want to tell me what happened?"

Fresh tears poured from her eyes, and no matter the size of her stature or her age, the presence of the Holy Spirit increased. "I told my mom I have to be baptized. She took me to the front, and I was so cold when they put me in the water. They prayed for me and put me under the water...." Her little voice broke, and a sob escaped her lips. "But under the water, the fire came all through me. I heard Jesus say, 'The light that shines inside of you will burn bright forever!' I have to tell everyone!"

I took her hand and led her up the stairs with her mother. Founders of Saturate Global and the hosts of the revival, Jessi and Parker Green, interviewed Claudia on the platform, and as she released her testimony, I watched the Holy Spirit move over the crowd, and many came forward to be baptized and receive prayer.

The Holy Spirit—through the words of a seven-year-old child again brought fresh revelation—opening our eyes to the power of the Gospel of Jesus. We prayed for Claudia at the end of her testimony and she was filled with the fire of the Holy Spirit. When she was able to get up, she helped us lay hands on her own mother to receive the baptism of fire. Her mother encountered the Lord with power as she never had before. The Lord then prompted us to call all children under the age of twelve up to the platform. Other children were also baptized in the fire of the Holy Spirit, and many parents and children were healed in that moment.

I knew in my spirit it was the commissioning of a generation. A generation who will embrace Jesus as the way, the truth, and the life and who have overcome death, having their spiritual eyes opened to the gifts of the Holy Spirit and the power and authority, of Christ.

What's Next Activation

With the help of the Holy Spirit, take a few moments to reflect on the following questions.

1. Where have I fallen into a pattern of talking about Jesus rather than spending time with Him?

2. How have I been relying on past information or even experiences with Jesus that have prevented me from new levels of discovery of who He is and who I am?

Journal the answers or simply sit with the Lord and note what is being highlighted.

— *Prayer* —

Lord, who can I help with this revelation of childlike faith with ongoing revelation? Make me childlike in every way. Keep me intimately dependent on You, growing in the grace and knowledge of You as I go but not forsaking our intimacy for knowledge about You. Holy Spirit, be my Counselor, my Teacher, and the Source of my life-giving revelation about Who Jesus is and who I am in Him. Bring Your illuminating light and heal my blind spots so that I will be able to see—to discern what is happening in the supernatural realms and to release Your supernatural life through me. Let my life pursuit always be about simply knowing You and doing as You have asked. Forgive me, Lord, for complicating the Gospel or for settling for speaking about You rather than desiring greater intimacy with You. Just like Claudia, let Your light inside of me burn brightly forever.

Give It Away

I believe we have an urgent call for this season to give to the next generation all that we have been given and to walk with them in order that they have the spiritual covering they need to accelerate their maturity in Christ. They are the ones who will bring in the great harvest.

What young people are around you that you can help lead into their own revelation as the Lord has done for you? If you don't have young ones in your life, ask the Lord to lead you to a place to volunteer where children need spiritual parents and friends. I have many friends who demonstrate the gifts and revelation of the Lord to children in secular areas such as recreation centers, after-school programs, or tutoring sessions. Every moment with a child is an invitation to break the power of sin and death over them and lead them into a heavenly encounter where they will no longer be blinded by the enemy but illuminated by the radiant presence of God.

Afterword

I want to leave you with one last thought. Psalm 103 is King David's song of praise. When you need reminding of all that God is and all that you are in Him, pray this! Sing this! Worship Him! He is worthy and your life in Him is glorious!

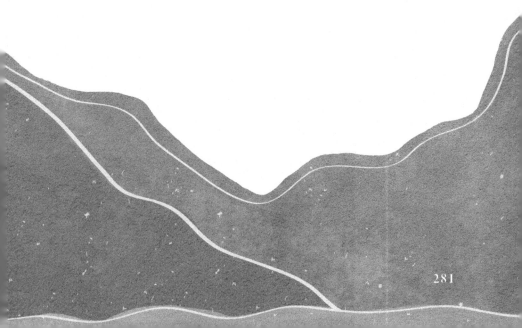

Bless the Lord, O my soul, and all that is within me,
bless his holy name!
Bless the Lord, O my soul,
and forget not all his benefits,
who forgives all your iniquity,
who heals all your diseases,
who redeems your life from the pit,
who crowns you with steadfast love and mercy,
who satisfies you with good
so that your youth is renewed like the eagle's.

The Lord works righteousness
and justice for all who are oppressed.
He made known his ways to Moses,
his acts to the people of Israel.
The Lord is merciful and gracious,
slow to anger and abounding in steadfast love.
He will not always chide,
nor will he keep his anger forever.
He does not deal with us according to our sins,
nor repay us according to our iniquities.
For as high as the heavens are above the earth,
so great is his steadfast love toward those who fear him;
as far as the east is from the west,
so far does he remove our transgressions from us.

As a father shows compassion to his children,
so the Lord shows compassion to those who fear him.
For he knows our frame;
he remembers that we are dust.

As for man, his days are like grass;
he flourishes like a flower of the field;
for the wind passes over it, and it is gone,
and its place knows it no more.
But the steadfast love of the Lord is from everlasting to
everlasting on those who fear him,
and his righteousness to children's children,
to those who keep his covenant
and remember to do his commandments.
The Lord has established his throne in the heavens,
and his kingdom rules over all.

Bless the Lord, O you his angels,
you mighty ones who do his word,
obeying the voice of his word!
Bless the Lord, all his hosts,
his ministers, who do his will!
Bless the Lord, all his works,
in all places of his dominion.
Bless the Lord, O my soul! (ESV)

About
Reverend Joanne Moody

Reverend Joanne Moody was miraculously healed of 14 years of debilitating nerve pain in 2014. She authored her testimony in her first book, *Minute by Minute,* and she is an ordained minister, a Master Equipper through CHCP of Global Awakening, and a Christian Life Coach through Western Seminary, and certified through the ICF. She leads healing teams, teaches, trains, and equips people internationally in all types of ministry venues. Joanne resides in Franklin, Tennessee, with her husband, Mike. She loves being mom to son Kian and future daughter-in-law Izzy and grandma to Parker.

Read Joanne Moody's first book
Minute by Minute

To reach Reverend Joanne Moody and learn more about
Agape Freedom Fighters, please visit:

www.agapefreedomfighters.org
email: Info@agapefreedomfighters.org

Looking to go deeper? The L.I.F.E. School through the Agape Apostolic Equipping and Training Center focuses on raising up believers to build kingdom families that run together to heal the sick, cast out demons, and advance the kingdom of God—freely giving away all that they have received from Him. Join us, and be equipped to hear God and move in the power of the Holy Spirit. Receive training to lead highly effective, apostolic teams. Experience Agape Freedom Fighters' family DNA, and step into the greater things that Jesus promised His followers would do according to John 14:12.

For more information on the
Agape Apostolic Equipping and Training Center,

www.agapeapostoliccenter.org